EUZKO GOGOA
(1950-1960)

Reimagining the Motherland

ZIORTZA
GANDARIAS
BELDARRAIN

Diaspora and Migration Studies SERIES #19

EUZKO GOGOA
(1950-1960)

Reimagining the Motherland

ZIORTZA
GANDARIAS
BELDARRAIN

**CENTER FOR BASQUE STUDIES
UNIVERSITY OF NEVADA, RENO
2024**

This book was published with generous financial support from the Basque Government.

Center for Basque Studies
University of Nevada, Reno
1664 North Virginia St,
Reno, Nevada 89557 usa
http://basque.unr.edu

Copyright © 2024 by the Center for Basque Studies and the University of Nevada, Reno
ISBN-13: 978-1-94-9805-74-1
All rights reserved.

Printed in the United States of America

Contents

Introduction xi

Chapter One: The Pillar Principals to Examine *Euzko-Gogoa* 1

Chapter Two: Historical Representation: Through the Utopian Preindustrial Basque Country to *Euzko-Gogoa* 7

Chapter Three: *Euzko-Gogoa* as an Allegorical Representation of the Rebirth of Basque Culture 21

Chapter Four: The Imagined Community Created in *Euzko-Gogoa* 49

Bibliography 113

Index 125

Notes for Readers

- Unless otherwise noted, the translations from Basque or Spanish languages to English in parenthesis are mine.
- The Basque names, words, and references are written as found in the source material.
- When analyzing the Basque Country, since the country is divided between Spain and France, the term "Southern Basque Country" is used for the Spanish Basque area that in Basque is referred as Hegoalde (South), and "Northern Basque Country" is used for the French Basque area that in Basque is called Iparralde (North). Four provinces shape the Southern Basque Country: Nafarroa, Araba, Gipuzkoa, and Bizkaia. The Northern Basque Country has three provinces: Lapurdi, Zuberoa, and Nafarroa Behera. The Basque Country is a small geographical area, totaling about 2,700 square miles. It can be said that the Basque Country has "one people, two states, and two journeys" (Ahedo 259).
- The term "War of 1936" is used instead of "Spanish Civil War."
- The following maps illustrate the location of the Basque Country with respect to the rest of Europe as well as the seven provinces of the Basque Country.

Notes
1. Irujo 2015, 225.

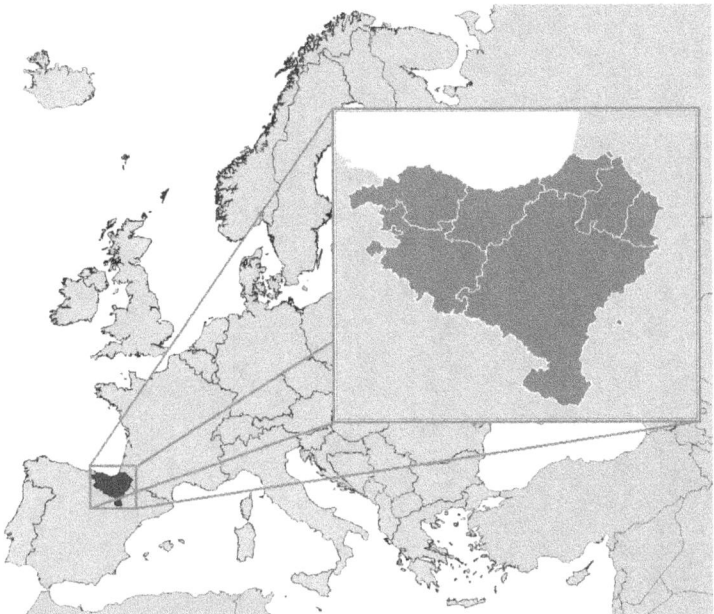

Figure 1: User: Zorion. "Location of the Basque Country in Europe." Basque Country (greater region), December 21, 2010, https://en.wikipedia.org/wiki/Basque_Country_(greater_region)#/media/File:Euskal_Herria_Europa.png

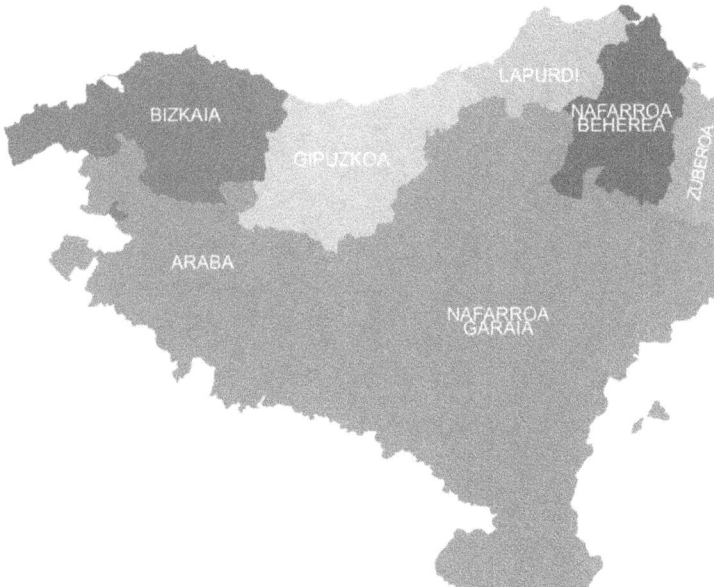

Figure 2: Fernandez de Betoño, Unai. "The Seven Provinces of the Basque Country." Basque Country (greater region), October 18, 2008, https://en.wikipedia.org/wiki/Basque_Country_(greater_region)#/media/File:Euskal_Herriko_kolore_mapa.png

Introduction

Guatemala, 1954. A black and white photo. In the portrait, dubbed "Euskal Hirutasun Santua" (The Basque Holy Trinity) by Andima Ibiñagabeitia, the three men are smiling in front of the Santa Mónica Residence in Guatemala City. It is a sunny day, the sky is perfectly, ominously clear, a perfect allegory of the calm before the storm. The three smiling men are the epitome of a generation of Basque writers. The image itself embodies an event, a memory, a history, and a literature. Perhaps this well-known image is the one that best represents the cultural magazine *Euzko-Gogoa* (Basque-Will) and its generation. To the left is Ibiñagabeitia, in the middle Jokin Zaitegi, and to the right Nikolas Ormaetxea "Orixe." In other words, the "Three Basque Quixotes,"[1] a paradigm of how it was possible to have a dream and how the dream ultimately transformed the Basque literary world.

Figure 1: "Picture of Andima Ibiñagabeitia (left), Jokin Zaitegi (middle), and Nikolas Ormaetxea "Orixe" (right)." In Guatemala in 1954.

After the War of 1936 and the ensuing years of dictatorship, Basque culture and language were condemned to disappear. The Basques fought on the losing side with the Republicans and were now under a totalitarian regime. It was in the darkest hours when those in exile took the lead in the fight for the survival and development of *euskara* (Basque language) and its culture. In the fall of 1949, Zaitegi wrote *Asmoa* (Goal), a brief report about his goal of creating a magazine that would be written only in Basque. Its title, "Euzko-Gogoa," has strong semantic and symbolic value because it could mean different things, all of them connected to the will, the course of action, the goal of the magazine, which gives it deeper significance. *Euzko* (Basque), a neologism created by the father of Basque nationalism, Sabino Arana Goiri, comes from *euzkera* (Basque) as *euzko-era* (the way Basques speak) and *Gogo* (Will), a polysemic word in Basque that has at least three different meanings. The first definition of *Gogo* could be "Soul, spirit; thought, mind, memory." The second one is "Will, the act of wanting." And the last one: "Intention, thought; purpose."[2] The magazine's title, similar to Zaitegi's "Asmoa," symbolizes the "will" of both himself and the Basque people to act on behalf of their beloved community, culture, and language. Specifically, the letter explained how the magazine was determined to awaken the Basque language, to promote collaboration among Basque writers, and through the use of language and literature to fight for the freedom of the Basque Country:

> Since we are abroad we are not using the Basque language as much as we should. The Spanish language is everywhere. Due to the war, under God's eyes the Basque people are spread all around the world and are about to lose the Basque language. Basque writers are silent. The Basque language has shown its value and strength in the battleground. The poets of their time fought in favor of Basque language and culture: Orixe, Lizardi, Lauaxeta, Loramendi, Yauregi, Barrensoro, etc. Some of them are not with us anymore. We want to awaken the Basque writers spread all around bringing them together. We are following the echo of the "Basque-Will" that comes from the north, south, east, and west. We know about the pure Basque town under the sunshine and the ones that are covered by snow. We want to spread and promote the Basque Will; the heart inside of the Basques, their shudders and fears. We have to go inside our heart and dig; the shell can be hard, but the inside is mellow. From now on, we only want to write in Basque; we want to gather all of the Basque writers and create the Basque magazine *Euzko-Gogoa*. Next year, in January, Euzko-Gogoa will be published. Goodbye everyone.[3]

During these years under Franco's dictatorship, many other magazines were published in exile; however, this book will focus specifically on the *Euzko-Gogoa*.

When Zaitegi founded the magazine in Guatemala in 1950, it was the first postwar magazine written entirely in Basque, excluding *Argia Euskaldunak Euskaraz* (The Light. Basques in their Language, 1946–1948).[4] *Euzko-Gogoa* focused on the cultural development of the language and created an imagined community or foundation for the future of the Basque nation through its writings.

Under Zaitegi's direction, the very best Basque writers in exile and in the homeland were brought together: Orixe, Ibiñagabeitia, Jon Mirande, Seber Altube, Telésforo Monzón, Federico Krutwig, Gabriel Aresti, and many others collaborated in *Euzko-Gogoa*. The magazine's main contributions were its belief in the linguistic capacities of the Basque language and its success in creating a bridge between the prewar and postwar generation of writers. Benedict Anderson argues that newspapers can change the concept of space and time and connect a community of readers who are spread all over the world (2006, 22). In this regard, *Euzko-Gogoa* represented the creation of an imagined community.

The cultural magazine *Euzko-Gogoa* was undoubtedly an emblematic leader in the history of the Basque press and a symbol of the resurgence of the Basque language and nation during Franco's dictatorship. However, very little academic research has been conducted on the contribution that Basque literature in exile made to the secularization and modernization of Basque literature, and even less research about the magazine has been published in English. *Euzko-Gogoa*, since its beginnings, played an important role in Basque culture. The symbolic, idealistic, and vocational understanding of culture, which was characteristic of the 1950s, created such a vital and dynamic movement that it is almost impossible to talk about the Basque cultural renaissance of the 1960s without properly examining this magazine.

The 1950s brought new hope for Basque literature, not only in the Basque Country, but also in exile. Although it was a turning point in Basque literature, it is a decade that has been generally overlooked.

Euzko-Gogoa was first published by those exile in Latin America, in Guatemala (1950–1955), and later in Biarritz, in the Northern Basque Country (1956–1960), where it ended its publication in 1960. Exile in the analysis of the magazine is being referred to as a forced migration for political and/or ideological reasons. As Paul Tabori (1972, 27) asserts, "an exile is a person compelled to leave or remain outside their country of origin on account of well-founded fear of persecution for reasons of race, religion, nationality or political opinion." *Euzko-Gogoa*'s journey in the Northern Basque Country would also be considered exile since Zaitegi was forced to leave his hometown in the Southern Basque Country and move to Biarritz in the Northern Basque Country. It was the only way to have the freedom to keep publishing the magazine.

The historical upheavals during this decade were unique and played a pivotal role in the redefinition of the Basque nation. In fact, the main pillars of modern Basque literature were established during those years, 1950–1960. After the loss of the War of 1936, the Basque government fought with the Allies during the Second World War, believing that after defeating Hitler and Mussolini the Allies would help to remove Franco from his position. However, the Cold War changed the world's course. Franco's totalitarianism didn't become the main enemy; communism took on that role. The global course of history drastically conditioned the future of the Basque culture and language.

Despite the global outlook, Basques worked to establish and promote their culture whether at home or in exile. Clear examples of their efforts include the creation of *Euzko-Gogoa* and the Basque publishing house Ekin (Charge 1942–). The scholar Gorka Aulestia (1997) states that Koldo Mitxelena, Santi Onaindia, and Antonio Maria Labaien represented a group of Basque writers in the 1950s who tried to keep the Basque language alive in the Southern Basque Country. Because of Francoist censorship, the War of 1936 couldn't be discussed in their writings, so their productions reflected the lack of freedom in the Basque Country (39). In the 1950s, the publishing house Itxaropena (Hope) and the magazine *Egan* (Flying 1948–) became the main Basque cultural platforms in the Southern Basque Country. Both institutions obtained the approval of the Francoist authorities. In 1949, Itxaropena published the poem *Arantzazu: Euskal sinesmenaren poema* (Arantzazu: The Poem of Basque Belief) written by Salbatore Mitxelena. In 1950, the collection of poems *Euskaldunak* (The Basques), written by Orixe, and the historical novel *Alos-Torrea (*The Tower of Alos), written by Jon Etxaide, were published. *Alos-Torrea* was indeed the first Basque novel published in the Southern Basque Country. These works were not a threat to the Francoist regime since their topics were related to religion and the traditional or bucolic Basque Country. In 1953, the Franciscans started publishing the magazine *Anaitasuna* (Brotherhood 1953–1982). In 1956, the Basque magazine *Jakin* (Knowledge 1956–) was created. Additionally, two significant meetings were organized to discuss the status of the Basque language. The first in Arantzazu, in the Southern Basque Country, organized by Euskaltzaindia (The Royal Academy of Basque Language 1918–) and the second in Paris organized by the Basque government. In this regard, the 1950s brought some changes to Basque culture.

Gorka Aulestia (1997) explains that *Egan* was the first magazine published completely in Basque in the Southern Basque Country (40). Although the magazine originated in 1948, it wasn't until 1954 that it began to be published only in Basque. (Previously it was a bilingual magazine.) The magazine was a literary supplement of the journal *Boletín de la Real Sociedad Vascongada de los Amigos del País* (Bulletin of the Basque Royal Society of Friends of the Country 1944–). *Egan* represented the urban and modern Basque world, always within the scope of Francoist limitations. The magazine's varied topics included poetry, literary criticism, Basque linguistics, theater, but never political issues.

In his book, *Euskal idazleak gaur* (Basque Writers Today), Joan Mari Torrealdai notes that the 1950s marked the revival of Basque literature (1977, 83). He asserts that *Euzko-Gogoa* in Guatemala made the awakening of Basque culture and its language possible. Martin Ugalde (1976, 245) argues that in Basque literature, exile marked the tone for change that brought hope and a platform for the maintenance and development of the Basque culture:

> The most important contributions of America to the Basque literature were the climate of freedom that allowed the cultural and political expansion of the Basque colonies and their economic development, two key centers: were the publishing house Ekin and the magazine *Euzko-Gogoa*.[5]

Basque literature awakened not only because of *Euzko-Gogoa* but also because the number of publications grew and because two literary generations began to merge. In other words, the 1950s became a reference point in Basque literature. It was the beginning of the modernization and the institutionalization of Basque literature.

What is clear is that Basque culture was dispersed and weakened after the War of 1936 but began to be rebuilt little by little during the 1950s. Nevertheless, when Basque culture is analyzed, the 1950s are still greatly overlooked, but even more so the culture created in exile that began gaining momentum during this period. The impact of exile was instrumental in the process of planting the seeds for future nation building. With a country defeated and its culture outlawed, it was in exile that the Basque nation could be rebuilt and reimagined. *Euzko-Gogoa* created a foundation of ideas that would serve to maintain the dialogue of a desired community while upholding and developing Basque language and culture.

Although it isn't the most analyzed decade of Basque literature, there have been publications regarding Basque works of the 1950s. In 1976, José Luis Abellán published a hexalogy titled *El exilio español de 1939* (The Spanish Exile of 1939). The third and fourth volumes deal with magazines of exile, culture, and literature. The sixth and final volume analyzed Catalan, Basque, and Galician literature in exile. In 1979, Joseba Intxausti wrote two articles about *Euzko-Gogoa* coinciding with Zaitegi's death. Intxausti suggested that Basque culture was in debt to Zaitegi (1979, 120). In the 1990s, the scholars José Ángel Ascunce and

María Luisa San Miguel edited *La cultura del exilio vasco* (The Culture of the Basque Exile), a book in which different scholars analyzed the impact of exile in the development of Basque culture. Another important work is Josemari Velez de Mendizabal's book, *Iokin Zaitegi*, a biography of Zaitegi published in 1981.

The scholar Larraitz Ariznabarreta also remarks on the importance of exile. In *Martin Ugalde: Cartografías de un discurso* (Martin Ugalde: Cartographies of a Discourse, 2015), she acknowledges the exceptional nature of the "experience of exile" and how it always reveals an obligatory reinterpretation of the personal identity in exile. Ander Gurruchaga argues that the biggest contribution of Basque exiles to the culture was a political attitude that rejected the Francoist system and brought continuity to the culture (187). According to Gurruchaga, the desire of Basque exiles was to link the old generation with the new generations to keep the memory of the past alive, especially in the political and cultural arenas.

Basque exiles maintained the nationalist code based on a traditional Basque nationalism in line with utopic preindustrial Basque society. Basque language, Basque laws, tradition, and historical peculiarity were the main ideas promoted.[6] Basque nationalism produced its own space, redefining its limits in exile. *Euzko-Gogoa*, faithful to the traditional nationalist ideals, tried to maintain the Basque Country by rebuilding Basque national identity, in other words, generating an idea of a Basque community based on the traditional, linguistic, and symbolic Basque world.

Research on *Euzko-Gogoa* did not begin until the twenty-first century. Up until this period, publications mentioned the impact of the journal but did not discuss it exclusively. The topics of exile, diaspora, and the repression of Basque culture are more commonly explored. In 2001, Paulo Iztueta published *Erbesteko euskal pentsamendua. Bi belaunaldien lekukoak: Euzko-Gogoa eta Zabal* (Thought of the Basque Exile. Two Generations: Euzko-Gogoa and Zabal), in which he analyzed the generational change in Basque culture through the examination of two magazines, *Euzko-Gogoa*, as a representation of the prewar generation, and *Zabal* (Wide, 1973–1976), as the allegory of the postwar generation. He also explores the similarities and differences of both magazines.

In 2009, Xabier Irujo published *Itzulpena erbestean: Bingen Ametzagak Ameriketan euskarara eramandako lanak (1938–1968)* (Translation in Exile: Translations by Bingen Ametzaga in America (1938–1968)) and *Homo Spelens: Bingen Ametzaga Aresti (1901–1969) Algortar baten bizitza erbestean* (Homo Spelens: Bingen Ametzaga Aresti (1901–1969) the Life of a Man from Algorta in Exile), in which he examines, through the life of Bingen Ametzaga, the impact of Basque intellectuals in exile, specifically in the United States, during the rebirth of Basque language and culture. One of the book's pillars is the analysis of the translations made in exile during the postwar years. And, indeed,

Ametzaga was one of the writers featured in the cultural magazine *Euzko-Gogoa*. Irujo dedicates some chapters to the magazine and to the intellectuals who worked side by side with Ametzaga to revitalize the Basque language. Likewise, in 2011, Pako Sudupe published the trilogy *50eko hamarkadako euskal literatura* (Basque Literature of the 1950s), in which he analyzes the disputes over literary language and the importance of different Basque intellectuals and the platforms used to promote Basque language and culture. He puts special emphasis on the figure of Zaitegi and *Euzko-Gogoa*, especially in the first volume. Finally, in 2013 *Jokin Zaitegiren ekarpenak euskal curriculumean. Eginak eta asmoak* (The Contribution of Jokin Zaitegi to the Basque Curriculum. What He Made and His Goals) was published by Jon Diaz Egurbide. The author analyzes the life and works of Zaitegi, particularly the relationship of his work and education. In 2007, this same author in collaboration with Paulo Iztueta published the books *Jokin Zaitegi: gutunak* (Jokin Zaitegi: Letters) and *Jokin Zaitegiri idatzitako gutunak I-II* (Letters to Jokin Zaitegi I-II).

Those studies provide a general cultural context as well as quantitative analysis of *Euzko-Gogoa*. They examine Zaitegi's character and personality, and they allow us to understand Zaitegi's ambition and motivation for creating a magazine during a decade of changes and difficulties. They provide strong historical background and information that offer the ability to further appreciate the impact of the magazine's creation of an imagined community in its pages.

The present study focuses on analyzing *Euzko-Gogoa*'s imagined community. It was in exile where Basque literature began to flourish. The War of 1936 and Franco's ensuing regime changed the course of Basque literature and culture. The repression and robust censorship implemented by the dictatorial government made any cultural manifestation in the Southern Basque Country practically impossible. Because of that, one can believe that *Euzko-Gogoa* was the allegorical representation of the cultural rebirth of the Basque nation, culture, and language. This study combines the texts written by Basque intellectuals related to *Euzko-Gogoa* and explores the magazine through different lenses, including those of cultural, national, and postcolonial studies.

In addition, it will analyze the historical background to show the importance of and the links between the historical context, Basque cultural institutions, and the magazine. The objective of this work is to further contribute to these previous studies to fill in the gaps and develop the significance of *Euzko-Gogoa*.

This study is divided into four chapters. Chapter one will introduce the theoretical framework and further examine aspects of nationalism based on the studies of Adam D. Smith (1992), Ernest Gellner (2006), and Benedict Anderson (2006). Anderson's theory of "imagined community" will be the center of my argument because he believes that culture is the fundamental pillar of the nation. The link between culture, nation, and nationalism is very important to understanding the contribution of *Euzko-Gogoa*. The chapter also analyzes postcolonial theory and cultural studies. The works of Frantz Fanon (2004; 2008) and Ngũgĩ wa Thiong'o (1986) will be used to analyze postcolonial theory. Referring to the work of Elizabeth Fraterrigo (2009) and Justin Gifford (2013) will be useful in examining the importance of new literary spaces for the reconstruction and redefinition of identities.

The second chapter investigates the historical framework of the Basque Country starting from the late nineteenth century to the early 1960s. The analysis of the historical events is important to understand how and why *Euzko-Gogoa* was created among the exiled Basque, and why it is the allegorical representation of the rebirth of Basque culture. A solid understanding of the historical context will also give a better understanding and appreciation of the magazine's literary content.

The third chapter analyzes Zaitegi's life with a special focus on his time in Guatemala and Biarritz, and it examines the connection between the author and his geographical space. This chapter will also develop a quantitative analysis of *Euzko-Gogoa* to demonstrate the number of issues, pages, topics, writers, etc. This analysis will help provide a better understanding of the identity and foundations of the magazine.

The fourth chapter is devoted to the exploration of the imagined community created in the pages of *Euzko-Gogoa* and its positioning of an archetype of Basque language, religion, gender, and nation. It will describe how the writers imagined the defeated Basque Country and how they reinforced a sense of collectivity among the Basques spread all over the world. That is to say how the magazine imagined the Basque nation and how it endeavored to rebuild it through its pages. To perform the analysis of the third and fourth chapters, archival letters and the magazine itself will be referenced. The conclusion will demonstrate how *Euzko-Gogoa* is a missing chapter in Basque literature and a magazine that goes beyond the "cultural" label.

Notes

1   Velez de Mendizabal 1981, 225; Iztueta 2001, 17..
2   Definitions from *Euskaltzaindia orotariko hiztegia*.
3   Zaitegi, "Gure Asmoa," February 1950, 8 (my translation).
4   Zabala 2016, 104.
5   My translation.
6   See De la Granja, *Nacionalismo y II República*. Beltza, *El nacionalismo vasco (de 1876–1936)*, and Gurruchaga, *El código nacionalista vasco durante el franquismo*, for an insightful analysis of traditional Basque nationalism.

Chapter One

The Pillar Principals to Examine *Euzko-Gogoa*

Throughout the ten years of its publication, *Euzko-Gogoa* created a unique corpus for maintaining and building an imagined community among its contributors and readers. This community served not only to cope with the struggles following the War of 1936, but also to combat censorship and create a space for cultural dialogue in hopes of one day turning the imagined community into a reality. With the Basque language as their cohesive element, they tried to rebuild the defeated Basque culture and nation.

The War of 1936 altered the course of Spain's cultural life, and therefore the Basque Country's too. The repression and the iron censorship implemented by Franco's regime condemned the "losers" to death, to prison, and to exile. Those who decided to stay in their homeland were condemned to a silence that, in the case of Basque literature, wasn't broken until the 1950s. Joan Mari Torrealdai, quoting Rafael Ninyoles, states that it was toward the mid-1950s when a new technocratic language policy began in which certain forms of cultural expression in nonofficial languages were tolerated (1982, 10). It was therefore from exile that Basque literature, culture, and language were revitalized and promoted. In the Southern Basque Country, Franco's regime imposed a policy of persecution of the Basque language that made any cultural manifestation in Basque impossible. In this regard, *Euzko-Gogoa* became a beacon for the Basque language.

To analyze the imagined community created by *Euzko-Gogoa*, Benedict Anderson's view of imagined communities will help to create a lens through which goals, accomplishments, and failures can be viewed. Other authors such as Anthony D. Smith and Ernest Gellner also assist us in understanding the nation-building process and the relationship between culture and nationalism. Moreover, to analyze *Euzko-Gogoa* as an imagined community, it is important to view the magazine from the scope of other theories such as cultural studies and postcolonialism that will help to further appreciate the depth of its content and influence.

Smith defends the importance of culture in nation building. According to him, nations and nationalism are not only ideologies, but a cultural phenomenon: "More than a style and doctrine of politics, nationalism is a form of culture—an ideology, a language, mythology, symbolism and consciousness" (1992, 91). For Smith, the key to nationalism is the creation of national identity, achieved through various pillars to form a common civic culture and ideology. What he promotes is the understanding of the cultural roots of nationalism, rather than cultural nationalism. To further explain his ideology, Smith uses the metaphor of Sophocles' drama *Oedipus*. From Smith's point of view, identity is not singular, but rather, there are "multiple identities."[1] The combined identities are those that constitute national identity. Therefore, various voices, viewpoints, generations, realities, and backgrounds are required to build a nation. In the case of *Euzko-Gogoa*, various authors from an array of backgrounds contributed to the magazine, which enriched the process of nation building.

According to Smith, it is culture that constitutes the essence of nationalism: "Nationalism is a *form of culture*."[2] For Smith, it is the intellectuals who propose and elaborate on the concepts and language of the nation, and through their musings and research, give voice to wider aspirations conveyed in images, myths, and symbols.[3] Smith identifies national identity as a collective cultural phenomenon. In *Euzko-Gogoa*, the intellectual writers were in charge of the maintenance and elaboration of Basque language and literature. Their aspirations are obvious in the magazine, in which the authors used literature to build their desired nation.

For Gellner, the formula for nation building consists of both power and culture. Industrialization brings with it the need for skilled labor, made possible thanks to education that transmits to all citizens a high culture with a unique and shared language. Gellner argues that nationalism arose because it fulfilled an important function and genesis for the modernization of society: "A man's education is by far his most precious investment, and in effect confers his identity on him" (2006, 35). One of *Euzko-Gogoa*'s main objectives was to further improve and develop the Basque language to a level suitable for academia and education. As will be discussed in chapter four, *Euzko-Gogoa* authors found it important to begin the process of normalizing various Basque dialects and promoting the idea of a future Basque university.

For Anderson, culture is a fundamental component of nationalism. According to Anderson, a nation is "an imagined political community—and imagined as both inherently limited and sovereign" (2006, 6). It is imagined because, although it is impossible to know all the members, each member can evoke in their mind the image of a communion among them. Anderson's ideas of an imagined community will be further used for the analysis and understanding of the communion created in *Euzko-Gogoa* for the maintenance of Basque culture. As Anderson states:[4]

> It is imagined as limited because even the largest nation, encompassing perhaps a billion living human beings, has finite, if elastic boundaries, beyond which lie other nations. It is imagined as sovereign because the concept was born in an age in which Enlightenment and Revolution were destroying the legitimacy of the divinely-ordained, hierarchical dynastic realm. It is imagined as a community, because, regardless of the actual inequality and exploitation that may prevail in each, the nation is always conceived as a deep, horizontal comradeship. Ultimately it is this fraternity that makes it possible, over the past two centuries, for so many millions of people, not so much to kill, as willingly to die for such limited imaginings.

One of the most important pillars of the nation-building process, according to Anderson, is language. He asserts that nationalism is born of the interaction between the cultural system and political ideology. Therefore, the "print-language" provides the necessary technical support to "represent" the imagined community: "Language has the capacity to generate imagined communities."[5] The development of print related to the ideas of nations and nationalism. In fact, cultural products—poetry, prose, music, and art—were used as a discourse. In short, the nation is conceived by the language; it is a community imagined through the language.

Anderson's ideology is useful when analyzing the goals and influence *Euzko-Gogoa* had on the Basque culture and nation. The network of writers allowed for the creation of an imagined community and a place of dialogue to develop a national consensus. *Euzko-Gogoa* was conceived with the notion that the Basque language written in a variety of publications would allow its community to survive and build its state, as will be further explained in chapter four.

When drawing on Anderson's theory of nation building, it is important to note the limitations of its use in the analysis of *Euzko-Gogoa*. The magazine was founded under Jokin Zaitegi, and although the works published in *Euzko-Gogoa* were quite heterogeneous and allowed for a variety of writers, it was ultimately Zaitegi's project.

From the scholar Justin Gifford's (2013, 99) point of view, literature is the perfect platform to create new spaces: "The novels of the 1970s push the genre of black crime literature in new directions by providing utopian resolutions to spaces of white containments." It gives the readers and writers an unequaled location to create something unique, as well as a place to think, rethink, define, and redefine its attitude toward the world. *Euzko-Gogoa* created a space where Basque culture could be forged. The object of *Euzko-Gogoa* was to provide an imagined community, separate from the Basque Country's cultural reality.

Elizabeth Fraterrigo (2009, 26) argues that "*Playboy* emerged as a contestant in an ongoing dialogue about a society in transition." It was the representation of a new generation eager to overturn the old order in the United States. *Playboy* represents a transition in society inspired by a new generation. *Euzko-Gogoa* was also a space for change in an imagined, written community. This was a space where the ideas of two generations could converge. The magazine was a platform for their goal of creating a reality out of their imagined community. Fraterrigo and Gifford both show how marginalized communities that don't necessarily have a current forum in society can use literature or magazines to create a space that allows for the reconsideration of new voices and an expanded canon. Similarly, *Euzko-Gogoa* represents a unique opportunity to rewrite the locus of Basque literature since exile offered a way of escape from an oppressed culture in its country of origin. During the time of Franco's dictatorship, Spanish culture and language were imposed on the Southern Basque Country. The Basque language was forbidden, and its use was punishable by law. In this sense, the recourse to postcolonial theory will address the situation of the "internal-colonialism" that occurred during Franco's dictatorship.

Postcolonial theory, as a literary theory, analyzes the literature produced in countries that were or are still colonies of other countries. The theory addresses many aspects of societies that have suffered colonialism such as the dilemma of establishing a national identity, the articulation of their cultural identities, the perpetuation of an image of inferior being, but also the anti-colonial revolts through the literature. Postcolonialism analyzes the psychological dimension of the relationship between the colonial author and the metropolitan literary tradition. Postcolonial theory studies the relations of the culture and the empire, as well as the resistance to the empire in the textual and symbolic field.

Frantz Fanon (2008, 9) argues that the colonized cultures themselves have been constructed culturally and subjectively through the internalization of the forms of inferiority advocated from colonizers themselves. For example, the inferior status that the colonizers attributed to the native language while promoting their own as the language of civilization was a key factor in understanding why the colonized adapted the speech and writing styles of the colonizer. However, Fanon found that in order to reject this imposition and reverse the situation, literature would be required as a powerful weapon of emancipation and dis-alienation.[6]

Fanon seems to openly endorse the idea that literature must engage itself in the task of bringing the community to a point of reflection and intervention. Fanon (2004, 188) states "the cultural obliteration is made by the negation of national reality, a national culture in underdeveloped countries should therefore take its place at the very heart of the struggle for freedom." Fanon wants to create a resistance against the ambivalent power dynamic between the empire and colony that affects the colonized through national literature. Fanon argues that national culture under colonial domination is a culture under interrogation whose destruction is sought systematically.[7] To stop this destruction, the people must wake up and literature must shake them and awaken them. Because if the colonized do not write their own story, they are condemned to immobility and silence.[8] Zaitegi and the contributors of *Euzko-Gogoa* also shared this mentality. Using literature and their words, they were combatants who fought to maintain and develop their nation and culture.

Ngũgĩ wa Thiong'o speaks about the importance of language and the connection it has with the culture and identity of a country. This Kenyan author (1986, 4) argues that to eradicate colonialism and obtain cultural freedom, it is necessary to write in the mother tongue by renouncing the language of the empire. For Thiong'o, native languages have the identity and expressive capacity of the colonized; and through them is the only way to achieve decolonization. Thiong'o states that language is not merely a string of words: "It has a suggestive magical power."[9]

Thiong'o observes that languages imposed by colonizers try to break the native souls.[10] He argues that colonizers devalue the native language and its speakers, trying to associate the native language with low status, humiliation, corporal punishment, and slow-footed intelligence. This breaks the dual character of language, which is on the one hand a communicative tool and on the other a cultural carrier: "The domination of people's language by the languages of the colonising nations was crucial to the domination of the mental universe of the colonised."[11] Language is one of the strongest identity signals. It is an inseparable tool of any human community that makes them specific of a character, of a specific history, and a specific relationship with the world.[12] Thus, when a language is erased, its culture falls into the abyss of the forgotten. The decolonization is therefore carried out through a linguistic policy in which the native language—a symbol of the spirit and soul of a people—must be recovered.

Culture, language, and politics (power) constitute the pillars of the nation. Intellectuals play a predominant role, and in this sense *Euzko-Gogoa* represents the intellectual elite that was responsible for the maintenance and development of the Basque language, Basque literature, and Basque identity. As Irujo and Urrutia (2009, 9) state, "the history of Basque language in the last 220 years has been plagued by prohibitions and political persecution." That is why politics (power), culture, and language are intrinsically connected in achieving the construction of a nation.

Notes

1 De la Granja, *Nacionalismo y II República*, 3.
2 De la Granja, *Nacionalismo y II República*, 91.
3 De la Granja, *Nacionalismo y II República*, 92.
4 De la Granja, *Nacionalismo y II República*, 7.
5 De la Granja, *Nacionalismo y II República*, 133.
6 De la Granja, *Nacionalismo y II República*, 25.
7 De la Granja, *Nacionalismo y II República*, 171.
8 De la Granja, *Nacionalismo y II República*, 31.
9 De la Granja, *Nacionalismo y II República*, 11.
10 De la Granja, *Nacionalismo y II República*, 9.
11 De la Granja, *Nacionalismo y II República*, 16.
12 De la Granja, *Nacionalismo y II República*, 13.

Chapter Two

Historical Representation

Through the Utopian Preindustrial Basque Country to Euzko-Gogoa

Before the publication of *Euzko-Gogoa*, decades of events shaped the political, cultural, and linguistic reality of the Basque Country. Historical upheavals influenced the ideology and mindset of Jokin Zaitegi and the collaborators of the magazine. Various predecessors shared fundamental beliefs and goals with *Euzko-Gogoa*, especially in the preservation of Basque language and culture. To understand the objectives behind the magazine, it is essential to examine the historical events that took place leading up to its publication. Namely, the Second Carlist War, Sabino Arana's nationalist views, the Basque Renaissance, the War of 1936, and the exile experience. This chapter will shed light on *Euzko-Gogoa*'s main purpose of creating a magazine to stimulate Basque culture and promote the Basque language.

Before the Second Carlist War in 1876, the demographics of the Basque Country began to change. The Basque Country experienced an industrial revolution in which major cities such as Bilbao had a large influx of immigrants from various regions of Spain because of the demand for labor. This migration began to change the Basque Country's reality. Larger cities began to emerge and replace rural lifestyles. With this change in demographics came new ideologies, religious beliefs, and the increased use of the Spanish language. Working-class immigrants, many of them socialists and atheists, didn't share Basque dogmas, *Euskaldun fededun* (Basque and faithful). Belen Altube (2001, 17) argues that, at least until the second half of the twentieth century, being a "good Basque" meant being a believer with strict adherence to Catholicism. This wave of immigration drastically changed the Basque Country's demographics: urban areas became more Spanish speaking, and the use of Basque was relegated to the rural areas. This created a polarization between the Basque and Spanish languages that many Basques saw as a threat to their identity and homeland.

Beltza analyzes the impact of industrialization in the Basque Country between 1876 and 1936. Although Beltza argues that the number of Basque speakers in the 1930s was randomly collected data, upon further analysis of the data in table 1, one can extrapolate the fact that the number of inhabitants went up, but not the number of Basque speakers. Farmers and fishermen used Basque as a vehicular language as opposed to the commercial and industrial workers who used Spanish. Beltza (1974, 2018) states that "Spanish is the language of the capitalist system and Basque is that of the pre-capitalist system."[1] In short, social, economic, and political relations were linked to the Spanish language, with Basque linked to farmers and fishermen.

Southern Basque Regions 1931	Inhabitants	Basque Speakers
Araba	104,176	10,000
Navarre	345,883	80,000
Gipuzkoa	302,329	N/A
Bizkaia	485,205	N/A
Total	1,237,593	N/A

Table 1: The Number of Basque speakers in the Basque Country in 1931.[2]

With these changes in society, many people began to view Basque as an inferior language. It became marginalized and was treated as an uncultivated language for illiterate people. Martin Ugalde (1966, 100) notes that Basque intellectuals such as Miguel de Unamuno in 1901 promoted the idea that "Basque is an inferior language."[3] His argument was that the Basque language wasn't a literary and cultured language, and as a result it wouldn't resist the clash with a stronger language like that of Castilian Spanish.

Some Basque intellectuals disputed Unamuno's hypothesis. These individuals also had a significant impact on the Basque Renaissance (1876–1936) that emerged from the end of the Second Carlist War in 1876. Resurrección María de Azkue, Arturo Campión, and Sabino Arana, among others, worried about the Basque language as they saw it as the national language of the Basques and therefore the sublime expression of their spirit. These intellectuals wanted to break with the stereotypes imposed on the Basque language in which Basque was defined as a rural language with no literary tradition. The Basque academic Jean Haritschelhar states (1991, 11):

> In the beginning of the new century, there are young people, Azkue, Urkijo, Arana Goiri ... who, after "The Congress of Basque Tradition," realized the importance of unifying the Basque language and the importance of the materialization of Basque studies, and gave birth to a new life.[4]

Through the efforts of these individuals, Euskaltzaindia (The Royal Academy of the Basque Language) was created in 1918. Estibaliz Amorrortu (2003, 57) states that the goals of the academy were to regulate spelling, codify new lexicon, and enhance literary Basque. The Basque language has a pronounced variation and differentiation in its dialects. As Koldo Zuazo (2013, 17) states, the Basque language has five dialects and eleven subdialects. The first dialectal map of Basque dialects was made in 1863 by Louis-Lucien Bonaparte, the nephew of Napoleon, who classified the dialects into eight groups. However, current studies suggest the classification of Basque dialects into five groups. Hence, the standardization and normalization of the Basque language was one of the main priorities of Euskaltzaindia. A standardized Basque language would be able to span various institutions, universities, and publications, while allowing for the language to develop and expand.

The Biscayan linguist and Euskaltzaindia's first director, Resurrección María de Azkue (1864–1951), was the main axis and promoter of the academy. Jurgi Kintana explains that Euskaltzaindia was founded without the support of various social authorities. Some supporters of the Euzko Alderdi Jeltzalea-Partido Nacionalista Vasco, EAJ-PNV (The Basque Nationalist Party, 1895–) were in favor of Euskaltzaindia and Azkue's project to invigorate the Basque language. Detractors, including those who were pro-Arana, didn't support the academy and its proposals for the standardization of the Basque language (2008, 35). The relationship between Azkue and Arana was tense, given their different approaches to Basque language and culture. Almost without exception, the nationalist writers followed the language model that Arana had advocated, with its orthographic system, a purist version of the language that replaced Latin roots with neologisms and a safeguard of Basque dialects, especially the Biscayan dialects. The followers of Azkue, on the other hand, advocated another orthographic model; they were not so purist in the lexical aspect and advocated the creation of a unified literary dialect.

Azkue proposed the use of enhanced Gipuzkoan as the basis for literary Basque, while using other dialects to enrich it. Since Gipuzkoa is geographically central, it was thought to be the easiest for speakers of other dialects to understand. Mari Jose Olaziregi states that Azkue did prodigious work on the consolidation of Basque studies, especially in the area of philology: his *Diccionario Vasco-Español-Francés* (Basque-Spanish-French Dictionary, 1905–6), as well as the *Morfología Vasca* (Basque Morphology, 1923), the ethnographic collections of the *Cancionero Vasco* (Collection of Basque Verse, 1922), and *Euskalerriaren yakintza* (The Knowledge of the Basque Country), and with the *Literatura Popular del País Vasco* (Popular Literature of the Basque Country, 1935–47) were crucial for investigative work in ethnography and philology and for the standardization of the Basque language (*Basque Literary History*, 141). Azkue's work was very influential in *Euzko-Gogoa*, with the magazine's director Zaitegi promoting his literary form of Basque.

Among the protagonists advancing Basque culture, language, and politics of this period, Arana served as a figurehead of the movement. In 1895, he founded EAJ-PNV. His main objective centered on the formulation and dissemination of nationalist ideology. His anthem, "Jaungoikoa eta Lagi-Zarrak" (God and the Old Laws), explained the religious and nationalist foundations of his political ideology. As Iztueta argues, for Arana, the identity of the Basque Country and its people was based upon the elements of race, language, customs, and historical identity (1991, 231). The Basque nationalist discourse was marked by the feelings of a defeated people in successive Carlist Wars who were fighting for the *fueros* (the old Basque laws, local laws forming a sort of civic agreement) mixed with religious sentiment, and who refused to accept a Castilian-based totalitarian national state. Arana (1893, 181) states that "Biscayans are not Spanish, not due to the race, neither for the language, laws or history."[5]

Arana's ideology and figure marked the path of the Basque Renaissance and the prewar generation. Arana inspired a deep emotional calling for the motherland, an unconditional love for the Basque Country. He also stands as a key figure in *Euzko-Gogoa*'s analysis of the situation. He is one of the main figures whom Basque intellectuals evoke to promote Basque culture and language. His ideas about the motherland, the conception of the Basque nation, and his linguistic purism are some of the fundamental concepts of *Euzko-Gogoa*, as will be seen in chapter four. Ultimately, Arana created the image and consciousness of "Euzkadi dugu euzkotarren aberria" (The Motherland of Basques is the Basque Country).

Although Arana was an important character in the development of Basque identity and nationalism, not everyone agreed with his ideas. Joxe Azurmendi describes how the Spanish Communist Party (PCE), among others, didn't see in Arana or in his ideology any positive features. The socialists believed that he was crazy, and the Spanish Catholic Movement (MCE) argued that Arana was the founding father of a petit bourgeois nationalist ideology, but not the founder of revolutionary Basque patriotism (1979, 18). Inside the Basque intelligentsia, there were those who did not share the totality of Sabinian ideology. Azkue, for instance, had mixed feelings about Arana. Azkue tried to consolidate the foundations of standard Basque language, but the extreme purity and the neologisms promoted by Arana were not overly appreciated by Azkue. Alfonso Irigoien (1988, 396) states that "the political conflicts in the nationalist world were following Arana's pathway, as well as in the linguistic sphere, and [Azkue] did not agree with that."[6]

During this time of cultural upheaval, women also began to play a role in politics and promoted the nationalistic preachings of Arana. In 1922, Emakume Abertzale Batza, EAB (Association of Nationalist Women 1922–23, 1931–36), was created. Authors such as Leyre Arrieta, Policarpo de Larrañaga, Miren Llona, Maite Nuñez-Betelu, and Mercedes Ugalde are the main scholars who have analyzed EAB. EAB had its precedents in the Irish association named Cumman na mBan (Women's League) established in 1914. The association was created in Bilbao in 1922 by women of the EAJ-PNV. These women went from village to village spreading EAJ-PNV's ideology, and more specifically, a woman's role in the party and in the community.

Larrañaga (1978, 45) analyzed the main objectives of EAB: "Disseminate Basque nationalist doctrine throughout the Basque Country, develop activities and initiatives in the cultural order, and develop activities and initiatives in the charitable and social order."[7]

To understand the role of women in the development of Basque nationalism and the creation of the imagined Basque community, the analysis of the EAB manifesto would be helpful in understanding the female figures of the prewar period that would thrive in the pages of *Euzko-Gogoa*. The manifesto lays out the religious, political, and social goals of the organization. On the religious front, women were seen as needing to instill religious and moral education in the home. Politically, women were seen as being responsible for the making of future patriots. They were to both preserve the Basque language and encourage their children to use it. In the social realm, they were expected to educate the family in the social ideas espoused by Popes Leo XIII and Pius XI. The party advised women to be submissive but not servile. After the War of 1936, EAB disappeared from the Basque territory to act only in exile.

During the nationalist movement headed by Arana and in conjunction with Azkue and others, several cultural events and organizations were born. In 1927, the society Euzkaltzaleak (an association committed to the development of Basque culture in the Basque language) was created in

Arrasate-Mondragón, Gipuzkoa, during the Euskara Eguna (Basque Day). As Lourdes Otaegi explains, it was an entity that promoted the most important cultural initiatives and activities during the pre-Republican years (1983, 20-21). Manuel Lekuona states that the motives behind the society were focused solely on the promotion of the Basque language while maintaining a politically neutral society (1984, 362). This mentality and political neutrality would be an important factor in the publication of *Euzko-Gogoa*. However, it was difficult for both organizations to be completely non-politicized and have no political undertone in their works. For example, in 1931, Nikolas Ormaetxea "Orixe" began to write the Basque national poem, following the wave of other countries. In his poem, *Euskaldunak* (The Basques), Orixe wanted to personify the living image of the Basque peoples' soul, with its legends, traditions, and folklore. Although the poem was completed in 1936, because of the War of 1936, it would not be published until 1950.

Although the Basque nationalist movement strongly campaigned to promote the Basque language, the use of the language was foreign in various intellectual spaces. Iñaki Aldekoa (2004, 129) states "despite the efforts of 20th-century Basque nationalism, the use of Basque in literary, journalistic and scientific works continues to be a minority."[8] Euzkaltzaleak worked to promote Basque language at a higher level of social and intellectual prestige.

The central figures of Euzkaltzaleak were José Ariztimuño "Aitzol" and José María Agirre "Xabier Lizardi." Aitzol and Lizardi promoted the Basque language through their poetry to grant it more prestige. Lizardi realized that previous styles of poetry needed to be revolutionized to reach the deepest knowledge of the language. Xabier Lete (1974, 16) remarks that "Lizardi wanted a superior Basque language, without losing its essence, but which may be an intermediary of the sinuous world in which we live."[9] Lizardi took *gipuzkera osatua* (enhanced Gipuzcoan) as the written form of the language, adding other dialects, words, and structures as needed. *Gipuzkera osatua* was the first step in the standardization of the Basque language. Lete states that "his poetry was difficult because it was expressed in a synthesized, thorough, complete, and renewed language; his language is the paradigm of wealth and precision."[10] Lizardi was the first to create a special poetic language in Basque. However, Lizardi's writings caused controversy in their time between critics and writers, such as Aitzol, who were more inclined toward "popular" writings. Actually, other members of his organization argued that his writings were too complex for the common man. Lizardi countered (1995, 122):

> Our written language is criticized because it is too elaborate. What a shame for them to surrender so readily, meanwhile we try to glorify the Basque language.[11]

Lizardi's main contribution was to elevate the cultural use of the Basque language. Otaegi (1994, 74) argues that "one of the major objectives that the organization *Euskaltzaleak* had under the command of Lizardi was to use the Basque language in culture and thus to honor it."[12] This mentality that Basque literature could become an instrument of national awareness and the promotion of a more sophisticated level of Basque language would carry over through the pages of *Euzko-Gogoa*.

Amid this cultural activity of the Basque Renaissance, the Spanish Second Republic was established on April 14, 1931. During its reign, the Basque cultural arena continued to flourish. Luis Villasante mentions that it was during this period that Basque literature began to establish itself. Books were published regularly, and there was a stable group of writers (1961, 312). With the Republic came one of the key figures of Basque nationalism, José Antonio Agirre, the first *lehendakari* (Basque president).[13] According to Beltza, the Basque political and cultural movement blossomed with the Republic, which gave it a more favorable atmosphere for their interests and needs.[14]

Despite the Second Republic's progressive beginning, it was shadowed in the end because of an abrupt turn of events resulting in the change of power under General Franco. The Second Republic was not exempt from what was happening across Europe, and its destiny was very much marked by the international economic crisis, the triumph of extremism in Europe with Hitler's victory in 1933, and the establishment of Stalin in the USSR. All these sociopolitical struggles radicalized the already tense situation in Spain.

During the elections of 1936, Spain was immersed in an atmosphere of immense social instability because it was polarized between two forces. The elections of 1936 gave the victory to the Frente Popular (Popular Front, a coalition of leftist parties). However, on July 17, the generals Emilio Mola and Francisco Franco initiated an uprising to overthrow the democratically elected Republic. The Catholic Church also supported the uprising. The EAJ-PNV was a decidedly Catholic party. Nevertheless, the EAJ-PNV did not join the military uprising and fought with the republicans. Actually, many Basque priests were imprisoned and killed because of their identity as Catholics and as Basques. Even though the EAJ-PNV was a Catholic and conservative party, it suffered the repression of the conservative and Catholic forces because it was also nationalist. José Álvarez argues that it was a conflict between the two versions of a nation that came from the nineteenth century: the liberal, secular, and progressive versus the conservative Catholic (2003, 461). In my opinion, these two extremes were equally dangerous because they shut out reason and avoided any form of compromise, preventing any productive result. This coup d'état was supported by other European fascist powers, such as Germany and Italy, who offered aid with their military support and strategies.

The War of 1936 represented a dress rehearsal for the Second World War, an unresolved conflict between the forces of democracy and fascism. According to Álvarez:

> It was a very complex conflict, in which there were international aspects (troops and armaments provided by Hitler, Mussolini, and Stalin), social (class struggle), cultural (secular Spain against Catholic Spain), various conceptions of state structure (tensions between center and periphery), confrontation between urban and rural Spain.[15]

The war produced thousands of Basque political refugees, although it has been impossible to confirm exact numbers of exiles who left the Basque Country. Beltza estimates that 150,000 to 200,000 fled the country. Also uncertain is the number of those who died, were executed, or were imprisoned during the War of 1936.[16] The Instituto Nacional de Estadística, INE (National Institute of Statistics), shows the population in the Southern Basque Country in the early 1930s to be 1,237,593, with approximately 12 percent of the population going into exile. During the three years of the war, the EAJ-PNV was characterized by its democratic and humanitarian role in the conflict.[17] In 1937, the *lehendakari* (Basque president) José Antonio Agirre (1991, 1) made his final message to the Basque people from Basque soil. In his address, he attempted to encourage his people, despite the imminent, inevitable struggles: "Our territory may have been conquered: but not the soul of the Basque people; it will never be conquered."[18] Iñaki Aldekoa argues that many Basques ended up in jail or in exile, in desperation and in silence, a silence which, with respect to literature, was not broken until the 1950s (2008, 149).

From its creation in 1939, the new dictatorial regime had several very ideological tenets. All political power was amassed in the dictatorship; the claim of the "unity of the fatherland" countered any political autonomy of the regions; and Castilian Spanish was promoted as the only language in Spain. Any peninsular languages or cultural manifestations aside from Castilian Spanish were forbidden and punishable by law. Gorka Aulestia (1997, 15) states that "one of the primary objectives of the new regime in the Basque Country was the disappearance of Basque language and culture."[19] Thus, exile became the only safe conduit for Basque language and culture.

Abellán recounts how those who fled the War of 1936 and the Second World War emigrated to various locations in Europe and Latin America (1976a, 15). Most of those in exile were well-educated, commercial elite, intellectuals, clerics, and upper-class Basques who found themselves forced to find a place in the diasporic communities. America offered the opportunity to reunite with family and relatives who had previously immigrated. The New World offered a familiarity of culture, and chain migration allowed these exiles to find opportunities while maintaining their cultural roots and language. Argentina, Mexico, the Dominican Republic, Venezuela, Colombia, Chile, Uruguay, Cuba, and Panama were all home to diasporic communities that hosted many of these exiles.

Ascunce states that, within Latin America, Mexico, Venezuela, and Argentina played a particularly decisive role in granting asylum to Basque refugees (1994, 27). As a result, most Basque cultural texts were published in these countries. However, other countries in South America offered a destination for clerics of various religious orders who had a great deal of passion and zeal for their culture. Nevertheless, the distancing of exiles from their motherland was a passive form of punishment and a purge.

This forced exile would last forty years, when some of those exiled were able to return to the Basque Country. However, many would never return. Some in exile, particularly those without any pending issues with Franco's regime, returned during the dictatorship. Those who remained in exile fought for the hope of the next generation of Basques, despite the separation from their homeland.

Although the Basque exile marked the rebirth of Basque literature and culture, the emotional and personal suffering endured by the exiles in having to leave behind their homeland cannot be forgotten. Gorka Aulestia describes the experience of exile with the emotions of isolation and dispersion, the problems of adaptation, the unknown time of return, the bitterness of defeat, and the nostalgia for the distant homeland (1997, 17). Although their love for the Basque language gave them the strength to fight for the motherland, the agony of the unsatisfied soul can last a lifetime. Exiles undergo a deep uprooting, and often do not find their place in a world where they cannot find a community for themselves. For that reason, decades later the Basque writer and exile Joseba Sarrionandia described the exiles as "apatrida" (stateless) since they don't have a point of reference. In the context of this sensation of limbo, they found in magazines a platform upon which to rebuild their lost nation.

Ascunce analyzes the uprooting and alienation suffered by exiles and the basic principles that define them. Exile reveals the tragedy undergone by the subject through two indicated principles: the geographical breakdown and the breaking of one's identity (2008, 37). The uprooting and alienation favor the creation or re-creation of an imagined or utopian story, which functions as the only way to survive the force of consciousness and loss or banishment. Ascunce remarks:

> The exile, aware of his physical and emotional deficiencies, recreates criticism or evocatively or politically struggles to reconquer the lost land and recover a personal history in the homeland. The validity of

this struggle presents, from the perspective of exile, the same value whether the means used for its realization are politics, critical study, creation or evocation. Any manifestation that takes as a reference the tragic reason of the expulsion, in any of its facets, is behavior indisputably symbolic of an exile.[20]

It was in the United States, the archetype of freedom, where Basque culture found the perfect space to grow. Jon Kortazar states that the first generation of the postwar period is a generation in exile (1990, 99). Exile became a fundamental pillar of the modernization of Basque culture. Edward W. Said asserts that modern Western culture is largely the work of the exiled, migrants, and refugees (2000, 179). These exiled individuals acted with pragmatism to survive, adapting their own identity to new spaces, times, and experiences. While integrating into their new environments, these individuals did not break off completely from their motherland. One way of maintaining their ties and identity was through newspapers, magazines, journals, and other forms of published media. The newspaper archive of the Basque diaspora, Uranzadi Digital, has collected a total of 136 exile and diasporic magazines and newspapers, with the majority from the late nineteenth to the twentieth century.

The Basque magazines published in exile and in the Basque diaspora before *Euzko-Gogoa* included topics related to homesickness, nostalgia for the Basque Country, sorrow over the War of 1936, the promotion of the Basque language, personal experiences, and local affairs. They were not exactly intellectual magazines, but more popular magazines. However, the intention of *Euzko-Gogo* was to promote sophisticated Basque culture, something new in the Basque cultural reality of those years. In fact, *Euzko-Gogoa* collaborated with the best Basque writers who maintained an almost unattainable level of literary perfection. *Euzko-Gogoa* can be described as an innovative literary product in the Basque cultural arena of the 1950s.

One of the first Basque magazines published outside of the Basque Country, *Californiako Eskual Herria* (The Basque Country of California, 1893–1898), was founded by Jean Pierre Goytino in Los Angeles in 1893. The weekly newspaper was the first to be written entirely in the Basque language in the United States. At the end of the nineteenth century, approximately five thousand Basques were living in California. The magazine's aim was to preserve a connection among the population while maintaining the use of the Basque language. As Xipri Arbelbide argues, like many promoters of Basque culture, language was the cornerstone of Basque identity; the strength of this identity is a result of this "sacred" language (2003, 50). In a time in which Basque people were still settling in the American West, the Basque language had to continue since it was the main symbol of the Basques, and it needed to be spread and strengthened in every corner of the United States. Goytino's work was truly patriotic, and it sought to unite the Basque diasporic community.

In the diasporic communities, both migrant and exile, magazines have been the link between Basque culture and the Basque people. Arbelbide states that *Californiako Eskual Herria* had more than three thousand subscribers in America and about five hundred in the Basque Country.[21] Matthew Jacobson (1995, 56) argues that newspapers are important transnational and diasporic elements: "Immigrant journals redressed isolation and bridged trans-atlantic distances by defining and addressing their readers as members of a cohesive diaspora community." In migrant communities, especially during times of war, Jacobson finds that nationalism was a powerful component and a frequent topic of discussion. The Basque media overseas (written in Basque and/or French and/or Spanish) was necessary to maintain the concept of belonging. In fact, newspapers were an important tool to promote and unify the fundamentals of the nation, to provide freedom of expression, and to raise people's spirits. As Benedict Anderson mentions, when print-capitalism arrived on the scene, language moved into the marketplace of generating imagined communities.[22]

With the loss of the War of 1936 and the following years of censorship under Franco, those exiled became immersed in the diasporic population. Publications became more than a simple bridge to "everyday life events" but now a space to maintain, develop, and enrich their culture. The magazines that were published during the War of 1936 while in exile condemned the war and tried to evoke patriotism among Basque communities in the diaspora and in the Basque Country. Such magazines include *Euzko-Enda* (Basque Race, Northern Basque Country 1939–1940), *Aberri Aldez* (For the Motherland, Mexico 1937), and *Nación Vasca* (Basque Nation, Argentina 1924–1940). Although *Nación Vasca* was founded before the War of 1936, Miren Barandiaran states that it was the only official publication that EAJ-PNV had in America during the war (37). After the War of 1936, a variety of magazines besides *Euzko-Gogoa* were published in exile during Franco's dictatorship. Most of them were nationalistic, carrying the view and arguments of EAJ-PNV. For example: *Aberri* (Motherland, Mexico 1946–1947), *Acción Nacionalista* (Nationalist Action, Caracas 1966), *Basques* (The Basques, New York 1943–1944), *Branka* (Prow, Buenos Aires 1967), *Euzko-Deya* (The Basque Call, published in Paris, Buenos Aires, and Mexico), *Gernika* (Gernika, Northern Basque Country-Buenos Aires 1945–1953), *Gudari* (Basque Soldier, Caracas 1961), *Erri* (Country, Caracas 1949), *Irrintzi* (Basque Scream "Neigh," Caracas 1958–1962), among others. Their main objective was to disseminate Basque culture, unite the globally dispersed Basque population, preach the doctrine of the EAJ-PNV, advocate for the idea of a free Basque Country, create bonds of solidarity, and promote Basque nationality.

Within the framework of the culture of exile, literature played an important role as transmitters of ideology, transoceanic movement of culture, knowledge, publications, and language. Martin Ugalde analyzed these first publications, arguing that they symbolized the blossoming of Basque literature after a decade of erasure. In 1943, Ugalde's book *Xabiertxo* (Little Xavier) was reprinted in Buenos Aires; it was originally published in the Southern Basque Country in 1925. In 1945, in Guatemala, Zaitegi published a Basque translation of Henry Wadsworth Longfellow's *Evangeline*. *Urrundik* (From Afar), written by Telésforo de Monzón, was published that same year in Mexico. In 1946, three works were published. Two were written by Zaitegi and printed in Mexico. The third, *Joanixio* (Johnny) by Joseba Andoni Irazusta, was edited in Buenos Aires by the publishing house Ekin (Charge), which was founded in 1942 (El exilio en la literatura vasca, 235–239).

After a long convalescence when the Basque language and culture were forbidden in the Basque Country, it was in the 1950s when the Basque culture began to awaken in exile. Torrealdai described this rebirth as "a shy awakening:" after a long period of silence, literature began to flourish little by little (1998, 39). *Euzko-Gogoa* was created during this period and became a leader in the rebirth of Basque language and culture through its works. With the collaboration of its writers, the magazine created an intellectual alliance that formed a resistance against the Basque cultural genocide and censorship happening in Spain. It was the first step for the rebirth of the Basque culture and language from across the Atlantic. This magazine was the first postwar magazine written entirely in Basque. Within its pages, writers in exile and in the Basque Country, from the prewar and postwar generations, would work together to create an imagined community, a transnational network, and a space of cultural currents.

Said describes exile as a scar that can't be healed, imposed between a human being and their native place (179).[23] This wound is impossible to cure; the achievements made in exile can't close it. As was the case for many other exiles, Zaitegi was always enshrouded by the loss of his homeland. In 1951, Andima Ibiñagabeitia wrote a letter to Zaitegi about the harshness of exile: "Those of us who are exiled are condemned to be wandering aimlessly from one place to another surrounded by enemies."[24]

Euzko-Gogoa represents the utopian paradigm of exile: rupture and distancing from the natural environment because of a forced action on the individual subject or collective subject; uprooting and alienation; vindication of the lost country (objective or emotional); and ideological commitment.[25] It seems reasonable to maintain that Zaitegi, from the antipodes of the Basque Country, played a predominant role in the Basque cultural scene. Bringing together Basque writers scattered across the world to unite and mobilize public and official opinion abroad and in the Basque country in favor of Basque culture. I believe that Zaitegi was a revolutionary intellectual forged in exile. Through the pages of *Euzko-Gogoa*, connections were created among writers and readers. They were able to share ideologies, interests, perspectives, and more. Zaitegi contributed to the creation of an imagined community that influenced the perception of what a Basque nation could be.

This cultural effort was not only limited to writers. The Basque government (mainly the Basque president Agirre), as well as other delegations and groups, promoted and participated in this effort with different types of contributions. For example, *Eresoinka* (Singing with footsteps), a multidisciplinary group of artists who were escaping from the War of 1936 in Sare (Northern Basque Country), became a cultural embassy of peace to share Basque culture all around Europe through dance, art, and music.[26] *Eresoinka* became a transnational cultural movement formed by two hundred Basque women and men specializing in various aspects of Basque culture. The main point of these cultural resistance and promotional works was to keep alive and unite the Basque community, as well as promote solidarity from other cultures and countries. Basque culture became the main tool of the Basque government in its worldwide diplomacy. *Euzko-Gogoa* could be included in the same strategy and atmosphere, as a tool to promote national identity and culture.

In its contribution to these efforts, the Basque government organized the first Basque World Congress in Paris in 1956. The Basque World Congress brought together people from the Basque Country, from the diaspora, and those exiled with the aim of proposing a future program for Basque society. The Congress sought to analyze the past, present, and future of the Basque people through different sections (1956, 13). It is remarkable to mention that this Congress was not only organized for Basques, but it had an international purpose, in which people of different nationalities and ideologies came together to discuss the future of the Basque Country. David Mota Zurdo argues that the objective was to revitalize the action of the Basque resistance, to foment its unity and to define a program of government in which all the political forces of the exile could participate (2016, 297). The Congress was organized in four sections: politics, society, economy, and culture. One of the main topics in the culture section was the status of the Basque language, in which Zaitegi expressed his concerns as well as his ideas for its development. He used *Euzko-Gogoa* as an example of a medium for the promotion of the language and proposed that other entities should continue to follow in its footsteps: "*Euzko-Gogoa* was an encouragement for everyone. And after its publication, many other magazines followed it by publishing their works in Basque."[27]

Euzko-Gogoa was a magazine published following decades of change for the Basque Country and its people. To understand the pillars of the magazine and the rationale behind its publication, it is important to know the historical scenario and context in which its creators lived and gave birth to its pages. Using this historical framework as a reference, the following chapters will analyze the accomplishments of *Euzko-Gogoa* and how the magazine itself influenced the following generations seeking to promote Basque literature and culture.

Notes

1. My translation.
2. Beltza. Nacionalismo vasco 1876–1936, (Ediciones mugalde, 1974), 10.
3. My translation.
4. My translation.
5. My translation.
6. My translation.
7. My translation.
8. My translation.
9. My translation.
10. Ibid., 21. My translation.
11. My translation.
12. My translation.
13. See Irujo and Olaziregi's book The International Legacy of Lehendakari Jose A. Agirre's Government for an insightful analysis about Agirre's life.
14. Ibid.,195.
15. Ibid., 461. My translation.
16. Ibid., 322.
17. Several studies point out this same idea. See Mota Zurdo, 25–75; Lekuona and Garrido, 135–152; and Arrieta, 52–60.
18. My translation.
19. My translation.
20. Ibid., 42. My translation.
21. Ibid., 54.
22. Ibid., 133.
23. Ibid., 179.
24. April 25, 1951, in Andima Ibiñagabeitia's letters 2.07.01 Gutuneria. KEH-0430-49936. Jokin Zaitegiren Funts Dokumentala. Euskaltzaindia. My translation.
25. Ibid., 43.
26. See Martija, Eresoinka: embajada cultural vasca 1937–1939, for an insightful analysis of the group Eresoinka.
27. My translation.

Chapter Three

Euzko-Gogoa as an Allegorical Representation of the Rebirth of Basque Culture

Jokin Zaitegi could be compared to the fictional character Don Quixote. He was a visionary, a madman, a dreamer, a wandering knight, but above all a believer. Zaitegi represents a dichotomy of character, a complex human who was forced to choose between his faith and his love for the Basque language: two antagonistic realities in a period where the polarization of individuals and ideologies was compulsory, without middle ground. He is therefore one of the most fantastic and interesting characters in Basque literature, language, and culture. In his dream to promote and develop the Basque language, he created against all odds a magazine written only in Basque and was able to distribute it internationally.

This chapter will describe the life and efforts of Zaitegi to bring to light an incredible and unique literary project that sought to enrich the Basque language and rebuild a defeated nation—through the creation of an imagined community. The quantitative analysis of the magazine will allow us to assess the achievements of Zaitegi and his collaborators. These will aid in further chapters when evaluating the qualitative results of the magazine. The challenges and failures of the magazine will also be explored to demonstrate not only Zaitegi's charisma but also the rationale for *Euzko-Gogoa*'s demise. After an analyis of Zaitegi's life, a description of the magazine will follow.

Jokin Zaitegi and the Beginning of *Euzko-Gogoa*

Jokin Zaitegi was born in Arrasate-Mondragón, Gipuzkoa, on July 26, 1906. When he was fourteen, Zaitegi expressed a desire to join the Society of Jesus and went to school in Durango, Bizkaia. There he grew close to his classmates Andima Ibiñagabeitia and Esteban Urkiaga "Lauaxeta," who also became key figures in Basque literature and culture. Ibiñagabeitia became his best friend and greatest moral supporter throughout his life. According to Gotzon Garate, after a year they all went to the Jesuit monastery of Loiola in Gipuzkoa. Zaitegi was there from 1921 to 1926 (2003, 4-5).

Those years in Loyola were critical to Zaitegi's relationship between the Basque language and the Basque Country. Jesuit scholar Patxi Altuna mentions that during Zaitegi's studies, the Jesuit community of Loyola was home to a renaissance of the Basque language. Zaitegi had the guidance of several professors: Father Apalategui, Father Olabide, Father Errandonea, and Father Estefanía.[1] These priests left a strong imprint among their disciples and were a remarkable group of *euskaltzales* (Basque language lovers). Several would later contribute to *Euzko-Gogoa*, including Ibiñagabeitia, Francisco Sarobe, Guillermo Larrañaga, Plácido Mujika, and Jon Goikoetxea. Many of them played pivotal roles in Basque literature and devoted themselves to its cultivation throughout their lives. The priests' passion for the language deeply influenced Zaitegi's own enthusiasm and devotion. Altuna claims that it was Estefanía, with his personal and literary qualities, who exercised enormous influence on several Basque students, playing a leading role in the enrichment of prewar Basque literature.[2]

Garate states that Zaitegi was the most vehement Basque language enthusiast, dedicating his whole life to God and the Basque language.[3] In addition to the influence and teachings of Zaitegi's mentors, his Basque cultural identity matured with the reading of the "forbidden" catechism, *Ami Vasco* (1906), written by Capuchin monk Evangelista de Ibero. The book discusses Basque nationalism and the Basque Country. The text contains the first ideological basis of the Basque Nationalist Party, the Sabinian ideology based on "God and the Old Laws" meaning Catholicism and the historical Basque independence based on *fueros* (the old Basque laws, local laws forming a sort of civic agreement).

With the support and the help of their priests, these Basque students created the Euskal Elerti Bazkuna (Basque Literature Association) with the goal of training future Basque Jesuits in the use of the Basque language. They also made their first collaborations and writings in the magazine *Jesusen Biotzaren Deya* (The Call of Jesus's Heart). Iztueta argues that one of the ideas that began to take root during those years in Loyola was the necessity of translating the Greco-Roman classics into the Basque language, with the aim of building the cultural pillars for a future Basque university (2001, 73-81).[4] Translations continued to be a major focus in the publication of *Euzko-Gogoa*, where the full capacity of the Basque language continued to be demonstrated.

Zaitegi later went to Oña (a Jesuit institution), in Burgos (Spain), where he completed his PhD between 1926 and 1929. Following their studies in philosophy, students were required to complete three years of mastery—often abroad. It is worth noting that some of the authorities in the Jesuit Order did not approve of the Basque language because they saw it as tied to politics. It was also very common in religious orders to send seminarians and students who showed an inclination and love for the Basque language to the Americas to separate and uproot them from their motherland. Accordingly, after studying philosophy, Zaitegi was sent to a Jesuit institution in Mérida (Venezuela) to complete the remaining three years of his studies.

After his stay in Venezuela, Zaitegi returned to Europe, and in 1932 he studied theology in Belgium. He spent three years there and was ordained a priest. As Jon Diaz explains, during those years, Zaitegi focused on poetry and translations in addition to his religious activities (2013, 86). After finishing his years in Belgium, his superiors sent him to the Jesuit seminary of San José de la Montaña in El Salvador. Zaitegi spent seven years in El Salvador and in 1944 he decided to leave the Jesuit Order.

Paulo Iztueta and Diaz recount a letter Zaitegi wrote to his mother: "As you know, Mom, I had to leave the Society of Jesus, because it was unbearable what I was suffering" (2007a, 100).[5] Zaitegi left the Order and he became a secular priest, unaffiliated with a religious order. With the War of 1936 and later the Franco dictatorship, the Basque language was proscribed by the Jesuit Order that supported Franco's rebellion. We must remember that the second Spanish Republic in the 1930s had strong laws against the Jesuits, and many Jesuits were forced to leave Spain. When Franco rose up against the Republic, the Jesuits saw Franco as a savior. Franco took advantage of the situation and changed the law in favor of the Jesuits; as Garate argues, the political-religious atmosphere became more advantageous to Franco.[6] The new institutional reality was unsustainable for many Basque Jesuits who suffered hatred and exclusion within the Order. Many Basque Jesuits felt forced to choose between their faith in God and the Basque language. Zaitegi chose the latter, but he never forgot his faith.

Zaitegi left the Society of Jesus in June 1944 following repeated and increasingly serious disagreements with his superiors. The outbreak of the war and the following years of dictatorship accentuated Zaitegi's differences with the Jesuits who backed Franco. This same year he settled in Guatemala, as Josemari Velez de Mendizabal (1981, 66) recounts Zaitegi's words:

> I wanted to go to North America, and I asked the Order to transfer me. The Basque president Jose Antonio Agirre was in New York and I thought I could be of good service to him. But the Order, instead of sending me there, turned a deaf ear and told me that my work at the seminary in El Salvador was irreplaceable. Later on, they thought that I could go to Idaho. But by then I had already contacted Arellano, the Bishop of Guatemala, who welcomed me with open arms.[7]

Zaitegi's arrival in Guatemala was immediately eventful. His Basque identity and his stubbornness were so strong that he entered Guatemala with his Basque passport rather than his Spanish passport. The Basque passport was an irregular form of documentation in the eyes of the interior minister of Guatemala. The interior minister unsuccessfully tried to convince Zaitegi to exchange his Basque passport for the Spanish one, which Zaitegi flatly refused to do. Then president of Guatemala, Jorge Ubico, also tried to convince Zaitegi to exchange his passport, but he could not change Zaitegi's mind either. From that day on Zaitegi had free access to the Presidential Palace.

Analyzing the sociohistorical framework of Guatemala, the academic trajectory of Zaitegi coincided with the Democratic Revolution of Guatemala from 1944 to 1954, also known as the "ten years of spring in the land of eternal tyranny,"[8] which ended with Jorge Ubico's tyranny. The importance of this specific space and time in Guatemala allows us to understand the creation of *Euzko-Gogoa* and its development. Guatemala became, by coincidence, a new space for Basque culture and literature.

Zaitegi had a very active life in Guatemala; he worked as a professor and as a secular priest. These activities would become very important later when he created *Euzko-Gogoa*. Those years became a turning point in Zaitegi's career since he was able to establish himself among the Guatemalan intellectual and political leaders and institutions. His position in Guatemala also allowed him to become a very good friend of Agirre, the Basque president in exile. Zaitegi's primary goal and commitment was to the Basque language; his political beliefs created networks and collaborations within the Basque government in exile. As Intxausti mentions, Zaitegi was an enthusiast of the Basque language, a patriot, and member of the EAJ-PNV (Basque Nationalist Party), but above all a devotee of the language.[9]

During his time as a professor and as a secular priest, Zaitegi developed the revolutionary idea of creating a magazine written only in Basque, and in 1949, *Euzko-Gogoa* was born. The driving force behind the project was the necessity of having a cultural platform printed only in the Basque language. In an interview with Josemari Velez de Mendizabal, Zaitegi mentions why he decided to publish *Euzko-Gogoa*: "During those years there weren't any magazines written entirely in Basque. I was tired of reading non-Basque language magazines."[10] *Euzko-Gogoa*'s biggest goal was to bring together the Basque writers spread throughout the world after the war, to rebuild the Basque nation, and to create a community of writers and readers. The magazine wanted to become the Basque cultural reference for the Basques dispersed in Argentina, the United States, Guatemala, Colombia, Cuba, Mexico, Nicaragua, Panama, Peru, Salvador, Chile, Uruguay, Venezuela, Belgium, Bulgaria, Denmark, Spain, France, England, Italy, Sweden, Czechoslovakia, Egypt, Philippines, Israel, and China.

On December 26, 1949, Zaitegi registered *Euzko-Gogoa* at the post office of Guatemala to be distributed across the world. Before the first issue was published, Zaitegi wrote an announcement, *Asmoa* (Goal), explaining the magazine's main purposes and amibitions, and shared it among the *euskaltzales* (Basque language lovers). Iztueta summarized that the magazine intended to be a meeting place for exiled writers, to recover Basque identity, to proclaim Basque as the national language, and to promote a Basque university[11] that would cultivate the culture and the language.[12] *Euzko-Gogoa* wanted to become the place where globally dispersed Basque writers could find a platform to write together. Basque literature was thwarted, and it was mainly from exile that Basque culture could continue to evolve as it had before the War of 1936.

The magazine required assistance financially and in terms of distribution. In 1950, the first issue was printed with an annual subscription of $10. Although Zaitegi invested almost all his savings into *Euzko-Gogoa*, it still wasn't enough to sustain the magazine. Its production was incredibly expensive. In 1952, to earn extra income to help pay for the costs of the magazine, Zaitegi opened his own school in Guatemala called Liceo Landibar. Even with the income from the school, finding personnel to help distribute the magazine was an additional challenge because of the censorship in the Southern Basque Country. Joan Mari Torrealdai states that the Basque writer Jon Etxaide was fined 5,000 pesetas ($40) by the civil governor of Gipuzkoa and jailed. Etxaide was taken to the Martutene prison and then sent to the Vitoria-Gasteiz prison for smuggling and distributing the magazine in the Basque Country (1999, 65). *Euzko-Gogoa* was immediately considered propaganda and a conflicting element contrary to the Spanish regime. Many tasks were required to successfully distribute *Euzko-Gogoa* internationally. To reach subscribers, entities, and readers throughout the world required an infrastructure that was responsible for networking between the magazine and its readers. The involvement of the delegates, the people in charge of moving the magazine, wasn't the same; some of them were much more involved than others.

Zaitegi began the magazine mainly by himself, overcoming many difficulties. He wrote most of the first issue in January 1950, using several pen names: Etxetxo, Ibartzabal, Urizar, Udalaizpe, and Izurtza. Luckily for Zaitegi, while reading the magazine *Oficina de Prensa de Euskadi*, OPE (the press office of the Basque Country, an official communication media of the Basque government in exile in the years1947–1977), he realized that the Basque writer Nikolas Ormaetxea "Orixe" was in Argentina. Orixe was at that time a literary icon and the cornerstone of the Basque literary world. Zaitegi saw in him the possibility of a productive collaboration and an enriching partnership for the magazine. Orixe could be a contributor who would give greater credibility, strength, and reputation to *Euzko-Gogoa*. Iztueta states that Orixe decided to end their partnership after six months because of irreconcilable differences rising from their equally strong characters.[13]

Although the collaboration didn't work out, in this short period of time the magazine improved a great deal, especially in gaining prestige. Txillardegi (1984, 31) wrote that "Orixe's word was Godly."[14] Thanks to Orixe, the magazine had the approval and credibility it needed for the Basque community. A contemporary of Lizardi and Lauaxeta, Orixe is the most important figure of the early twentieth century in the Basque cultural panorama and one of the most important authors of Basque literature. Orixe has left a copious amount of work in both prose and verse, both original and translated works. Juan Iñazio Goikoetxea (1972, xxxii) asserts that Orixe's success in the formation of new words—his precision and transparency in literature—is extraordinary. Within his literary production, his poetic work *Euskaldunak* (The Basques) and the essay *Quiton arrebarekin* (In Quito with My Sister) are the most recognized. *Quiton arrebarekin* was published in *Euzko-Gogoa* in ten issues between 1950 and 1954.[15]

After Orixe's resignation, Zaitegi was once again by himself. The management of the magazine, his work as the director and teacher at his school, and his duties as a priest were too great of a burden for a single person. He insisted that his best friend, Andima Ibiñagabeitia, come to Guatemala to help him with the direction of the magazine and with managing the school. At that time, the publication had already a certain identity, had developed its own linguistic and literary conventions, and had associations with more writers. By 1954, the magazine published nineteen issues, and fifty different writers were collaborating in the magazine. They included Jon Mirande, Federiko Krutwing, Jon Etxaide, Nemesio Etxaniz, Txomin Peillen, and Salbatore Mitxelena.

A Brief Description of *Euzko-Gogoa*

Euzko-Gogoa was a cultural magazine; its main purpose was the maintenance, development, and use of the Basque language. The magazine was a first step toward the rebirth of Basque culture and language from the other side of the Atlantic. *Euzko-Gogoa* rearranged the spaces and identities that were forbidden in the Basque Country under the Franco dictatorship. The magazine also analyzed and developed other areas of study such as history, natural science, religion, and philosophy. This section will describe from a quantitative approach the distribution of topics, political tone, demographics of the writers and subscribers, and the magazine's limitations.

Euzko-Gogoa was published during two different periods and from two locations: The first period of publication took place in Guatemala (1950–1955) in the Basque exile in Latin America. Latin America was one of the first geographical areas in which exiles, both Basques and Spaniards, sought refuge during the War of 1936. The second period of the magazine took place, also in exile, in the coastal town of Biarritz, in the Northern Basque Country (1956–1960). In Guatemala, twenty-seven issues were printed: seven in 1950; six in 1951; six in 1952; five in 1954; and three in 1955 with a total of 734 articles. During its publication in Biarritz, seventeen issues were printed: six issues in 1956; five in 1957; four in 1958, and two in 1959 (the last issue of 1959 appeared the following year in 1960) with 437 texts.

After forty-four issues, a total of 1,171 articles consisting of 3,658 pages were published with the efforts of 153 writers (five of whom were women) with the majority of the Basque writers of the time collaborating in the magazine. In 1960, the magazine ended its publication. Table 2 demonstrates the general quantitative data of *Euzko-Gogoa*.

Magazine	Year	Issues	Articles	Pages	Writers
Euzko-Gogoa	1950–1960	44	1,171	3,658	153

Table 2: Quantitative data of Euzko-Gogoa

Euzko-Gogoa's original intention was to publish every two months. However, this only occurred during three of the years of publication (1951, 1952, 1956). As stated before, the magazine covered a variety of topics and was divided into three main sections: introduction, body of works, and closing arguments.

The introductory section of *Euzko-Gogoa* was called "Ataurrekoa" (Introduction): 1954, (1–2); (3–4); (5–8); (9–10)[16]. During its time in Biarritz, the magazine maintained the introductory section, but it was called "Atarikoa" (a synonym for Ataurrekoa): 1956, (1–2); (3–4); (5–6); (7–8); 1957, (5–6); (7–8); (9–12); 1958, (1–2); (3–4); (5–8); (9–12); 1959, (1–2), (3–6). In the sections "Ataurrekoa" and "Atarikoa," the directors of the magazine, Zaitegi and Ibiñagabeitia, shared their ideology. The magazine continued to elaborate a discourse in favor of developing the Basque language. The editorial line implied that the Basque language was the cornerstone of the Basques and therefore their existence and continuation were connected to their language. Like the ideas promoted by Fanon, Zaitegi and Ibiñagabeitia also saw language as a form of dis-alienation from the colonizer, which could be used as a weapon of emancipation, as explained in *The Wretched of the Earth*.

The magazine was written by people with different ideologies, but with the same goal: to enrich and maintain the Basque language, and therefore the Basque nation. Despite their differences, all of them created an imagined Basque community from different political perspectives. As noted in chapter one, Anthony D. Smith argues in *National Identity* that efforts like those of Zaitegi are key in the nation-building process where various viewpoints and realities share a similar ideology to create a sense of nationalism. This nationalism is built on various pillars that are seen in *Euzko-Gogoa* such as language, religion, and gender. *Euzko-Gogoa*'s contributors shared a common goal of discussing, maintaining, and expanding Basque culture through its publication. By doing so, they could create a community or nation that was otherwise impossible in the Southern Basque Country. Following Benedict Anderson, we could say that this imagined community aimed to create a cultural, religious, gendered, and political conceptualization of Basque identity and the Basque Country in the magazine.

They also highlighted that the magazine wasn't part of any political party. Indeed, all these writers emphasized the idea that *Euzko-Gogoa* did not follow any political agenda. However, the magazine echoed the political and philosophical position of the traditional Basque nationalistic views. Most of the issues of the magazine included conventional Basque nationalist representations and symbology, such as the tree of Gernika, the *ikurriña* (the Basque flag), the *fueros* (the old Basque laws, local laws forming a sort of civic agreement), and the figure of Sabino Arana.[17] Remember the importance attributed by scholars to symbols, including Smith, who states how symbols are an important part of creating a cultural nationalism and can function in establishing the imagery of a country or community.[18]

While Zaitegi's main concern was the Basque language, his political ideas and inclinations are clear in the magazine. In fact, both Zaitegi and Ibiñagabeitia were good friends of José Antonio Agirre, the Basque president in exile. Agirre was described by Ludger Mess (2006) as a "pragmatic prophet." In fact, Agirre was a moral leader of the Basque diasporic community, and a common reference for Basque nationalism and the nation-building process.

The magazine wanted to open new avenues to provide innovative capacities to the Basque language. Through a variety of topics, *Euzko-Gogoa* sought the social normalization of the Basque language and showcased its linguistic possibilities:

Topics	Percentage of Topics	Percentage of Subtopics
Prologue	1.03	
Introduction	4.68	
Literature	57.48	
Poetry		10.7
Narrative		12.02
Drama		19.5
Reviews		15.26
Linguistics	14.43	
Sociology	4.15	
History	5.96	
Religion	4.71	
Fine Arts	1.59	
Philosophy	3.35	
Ethnology	1.47	
Natural Science	0.94	
Psychology	0.26	
Other	0.05	
Total	**100**	

Table 3: Topics of Euzko-Gogoa.

Literature and linguistics are the most common topics, with literature at 57.48 percent and linguistics at 14.43 percent. Olaziregi (2012, 139) states that the magazine represented the process of secularizing Basque literature. It is also interesting to note the relevance of the arts, sciences, and philosophy in the magazine, showing the inquisitive intellectual attitude toward questions that arise in life as well as demonstrating the literary capacity of the Basque language. As previously stated, one of Zaitegi's dreams was to create the basis for a future Basque university. According to Karmele Artetxe (2012, 36), *Euzko-Gogoa* was a project intended to use the Basque language to transmit high-level knowledge, a project to transform Basque language into a cultural language. *Euzko-Gogoa* was envisioned to use sophisticated Basque in different disciplines such as philosophy, psychology, ethnology, history, sociology, theology, etc. to have the Basque language ready (and materials in Basque prepared) for when a Basque university was rebuilt. This advancement in literary Basque language would also contribute to Basque culture and nation building.

Throughout the existence of the magazine, literary translations played an important role. The translations showed the linguistic capacities and wealth of the Basque language. Works written by Sophocles, Cicero, William Shakespeare, Charles Baudelaire, Paul Verlaine, Edgar Allan Poe, Selma Lagerlöf, Franz Kafka, Pío Baroja, Juan Ramón Jiménez, Jacinto Benavente, and others were translated into Basque. These texts lent increased credibility and support to the linguistic ability of the Basque language. As we will see in chapter four, translations created a corpus of works that helped build a foundation for literary Basque. Above all, literary translation had important relevance in the magazine. The idea was to internationalize the Basque language and demonstrate its linguistic richness. See tables 6 and 7.

On another level, social issues, to a lesser extent, found a space in *Euzko-Gogoa*. "Euzko-langilliei" (To the Basque Workers) written by Erraimun Argarate, was an article divided over six issues published between 1950 and 1952. The goal of the article was to speak about ELA Euzko Langille Askatasuna (Basque Workers Solidarity, 1911–), a union created by members of the EAJ-PNV (Basque Nationalist Party).[19] The article promoted the unionizing of Basque workers while making reference to Christianity. ELA is a Basque union rooted in the traditionalist and nationalist forces.

With the aim of legitimizing the Basque community, *Euzko-Gogoa* also offered a space for other individuals who did not belong to the Basque diasporic community to publish their own writings and in turn help finance the magazine. In fact, *Euzko-Gogoa* provided a forum for the Spanish speakers of Guatemala. The publications *El INFOP: esperanza de Guatemala* (The INFOP: the Hope of Guatemala, 1950) and *Hacia el futuro agrario* (Toward the Agrarian Future, 1954) analyzed the situation of the Guatemalan working class and farmers. One of the articles discussed how the Instituto de Fomento de la Producción, INFOP (Institute for the Promotion of Production), an institution created in Guatemala in 1949, operated in favor of the workers of Guatemala to bring to fruition the economic improvement of the Guatemalan people and country. The other article analyzed the benefits that Guatemala had experienced through the agrarian reforms made across the country. In this way *Euzko-Gogoa* became a portal for the social concerns experienced by many of the inhabitants of Guatemala.

The last section of the magazine was reserved for "Aldizkariak" (Magazines) and "Irakurlearen Txokoa" (Readers Corner/Comment Section). Ibiñagabeitia was largely in charge of these last sections. In "Aldizkariak," Ibiñagabeitia would mention other Basque magazines that were being published both in the diaspora and in the Basque Country, including the following (table 4):

Year	Title	Publication Info
1951 (9–10)	*Boletín de la Real Sociedad Bascongada de Amigos del País* (Bulletin of the Royal Basque Society of Friends of the Country)	Southern Basque Country: Donostia-San Sebastián 1945–
	Egan (Flying)	Southern Basque Country: Donostia-San Sebastián 1948–
	Boletín del Instituto Americano de Estudios Vascos (Bulletin of American Institute of Basque Studies)	Argentina: Buenos Aires 1950–1993
	Gure Herria (Our Country)	Northern Basque Country: Baiona (Bayonne) 1921–1976
	Alderdi Party (Politics)	Northern Basque Country: Baiona (Bayonne) 1947–1974
	Herria (Country)	Northern Basque Country: Baiona (Bayonne) 1944
	Euzko-Deya (The Voice of the Basques)	Paris 1936–1972
1952 (5–6)	*Aranzazu* (Sanctuary of Aranzazu)	Southern Basque Country: Aranzazu, Oñati 1921–2001

Year	Title	Publication Info
	Alderdi Party (Politics)	Northern Basque Country: Baiona (Bayonne) 1947–1974
	Eusko-Jakintza (Basque Knowledge)	Northern Basque Country: Sara-Baiona, (Sare-Bayonne) 1947–1957
	Boletín de la Real Sociedad Bascongada de Amigos del País (Bulletin of the Royal Basque Society of Friends of the Country)	Southern Basque Country: Donostia-San Sebastián 1945–
	Egan (Flying)	Southern Basque Country: Donostia-San Sebastián 1948–
	Boletín del Instituto Americano de Estudios Vascos (Bulletin of American Institute of Basque Studies)	Argentina: Buenos Aires 1950–1993
1952 (9–10)	*Gernika* (Guernica)	Northern Basque Country and Argentina 1945–1953
	Gure Herria (Our Country)	Northern Basque Country: Baiona (Bayonne) 1921–1976
	Aranzazu (Sanctuary of Aranzazu)	Southern Basque Country: Aranzazu, Oñati 1921–2001
	Alderdi Party (Politics)	Northern Basque Country 1947–1974
1954 (9–10)	*Othoizlari* (Prayer)	Northern Basque Country: Baiona (Bayonne) 1954–1986
	Euzko-Deya (The Voice of the Basques)	Paris 1936–1972

Year	Title	Publication Info
	Alderdi Party (Politics)	Northern Basque Country: Baiona (Bayonne) 1947–1974
	Euskalduna (The Basque)	Argentina: Buenos Aires 1954–1955
	Euskalzaleak (Fond of Basque)	Argentina: Buenos Aires 1951–1960
1954 (11–12)	*Egan* (Flying)	Southern Basque Country: Donostia-San Sebastián 1948–
	Euzko-Deya (The Voice of the Basques)	Paris 1936–1972
	Boletín del Instituto Americano de Estudios Vascos (Bulletin of American Institute of Basque Studies)	Argentina: Buenos Aires 1950–1993
	Boletín de la Real Sociedad Bascongada de Amigos del País (Bulletin of the Royal Basque Society of Friends of the Country)	Southern Basque Country: Donostia-San Sebastián 1945–
	Elgar (Together)	Paris 1948–2008
	Gure Herria (Our Country)	Northern Basque Country: Baiona (Bayonne) 1921–1976
	Zeruko Argia (Light for Heaven)	Southern Basque Country: Donostia-San Sebastián 1919–
	Anaitasuna (Brotherhood)	Southern Basque Country: Bilbao 1953–1982
	Aranzazu (Sanctuary of Aranzazu)	Southern Basque Country: Aranzazu, Oñati 1921–2001

This list reveals that *Euzko-Gogoa* reviewed and commented on other magazines that were being published during that time.

Finally, in the section "Irakurlearen Txokoa," usually published at the end of the issue, *Euzko-Gogoa* promoted discussion and dialogue between the readers and the writers. The topics varied, consisting of reflections as well as debates or polemics. This section was eclectic; many different ideas were discussed, including the magazine's aesthetics and accomplishments, Basque intellectuals who had died, information about Basque writers all over the world, and cultural activities in the Southern Basque Country: 1954, (1–2); (3–4); (5–8); (9–10); 1955, (3–4); (5–12); 1956, (1–2); (5–6); (7–8); (9–10); (11–12); 1957, (1–2); (3–4); (5–6); (7–8); (9–12); 1958, (1–2); (9–12); 1959, (1–2). This commentary section was especially strong during the magazine's second period, when it was published in Europe.

Although the magazine defined itself as a cultural entity and tried to "avoid" any political statements, Intxausti states that it had a political inclination, especially during its first years.[20] Mercedes Ugalde (1993, 578) affirms that *Euzko-Gogoa* was a publication with nationalist influence. The political identity of *Euzko-Gogoa* can be also appreciated by its covers during its two periods. The magazine had two different covers, one that was used when the magazine was created in the Latin American exile, and the second during its years in Biarritz. The publications in Guatemala had artwork with Basque political references shown below that was avoided in the later editions. Its size was 11.8 inches by 8.6 inches.

Euzko-Gogoa's cover page in Guatemala 1950–1955.

When analyzing the cover of *Euzko-Gogoa* during its Guatemalan period, one can see the significant nationalist symbols: the coat of arms, the mountain, and the sun, demonstrating Zaitegi's political affiliation. The coat of arms *zazpiak bat* (seven in one) represents the seven territories of the

Basque Country. Next to the coat of arms stands a mountain that appears to be Aralar. Aralar is in the heart of the Basque Country and has always been important in Basque mythology. The iconic mountain is a symbol for the Basque terrain. Above the mountain, a huge sun shines, symbolizing the poem *Itxarkundia* (Hope), written by Sabino Arana. This poem was also a nationalist hymn from the Sabinian period: "The sun of freedom comes out through the mountain / Its light is spread all around / Wake up Basques! / Hurray for all Basques! / Long live the old laws!" The sun reflects the symbolic universe of the Basque nation that in turn contributes to creating an imagined community in Guatemala with religious overtones. Jacques Blot (1984, 24) states that in Basque culture the sun has a special place, where the sun is "the light of day," "the eye of God." The sun of the Earth and its morning rays scare away evil spirits.

From the very beginning, the cover page was a topic of discussion among the readers. There was a desire for a more functional and durable cover with a cleaner look. The following excerpts from *Euzko-Gogoa* demonstrate how they wanted to change various characteristics of the cover page, ("Irakurlearen Txokoa" 1954 (1–2), 47), "Irakurlearen Txokoa" 1954 (11–12), 207):

> Arantzibia argues: "From my point of view the magazine should be smaller, 9 x 5.3 in; it would be easier to carry, I would also recommend a stronger cover to read it more easily." Yes, my friend, we are trying to do our best to improve our magazine; aesthetically, in its size, and for its content.[21]
>
> *About the magazine*—Many of our readers want to change the format and the cover of the magazine. They are happy about the content, most of them don't want any changes. They also suggest changing the name to make it easier to market. One of our writers also suggested different names for the magazine "Praise" or "Literature," the same person also suggested that we should remove the symbols that appear on the cover. We are happy to comply when what they ask is reasonable.[22]

As a result, during its publication in Biarritz, the magazine had a more neutral cover omitting Basque symbology. Contrary to the first cover in Guatemala, *Euzko-Gogoa*'s cover in Biarritz was more simple, colorful, modern, and pragmatic. The standard design of the first period of the magazine totally disappeared during its publication in the Northern Basque Country. It was also smaller, 7.08 inches by 5.1 inches. See page 36:

Euzko-Gogoa's cover pages, Biarritz 1956, 1958, 1959

Nevertheless, the beauty of the magazine was its ability to foster a collaborative effort among writers from a variety of social and professional backgrounds. It also was the bridge between two generations of writers. *Euzko-Gogoa* created a literary platform that promoted the endurance of the Basque language and also cultivated an imagined community. As previously mentioned, the decades leading up to the magazine were years of war that deeply marked the lives of many. Each writer brought to *Euzko-Gogoa* a unique view and background from their experiences during a time of global instability. Comparing the accomplishments of *Euzko-Gogoa* with the analysis of other cultural works discussed by scholars Justin Gifford and Elizabeth Fraterrigo, when referring to other magazines such as *Playboy* and *Players,* we could say that *Euzko-Gogoa* became a new space to promote and redefine Basque language and culture.

Euzko-Gogoa managed to have a collaboration of many well-known Basque authors, including those living in the Southern Basque Country. The authors of the prewar generation were culturally active between 1930 and 1936. These writers suffered the war, both personally and within their families. They saw how Franco's uprising led to the decline of the Southern Basque Country and Basque culture. Many of them went into exile for protection. Those who stayed in the Southern Basque Country suffered different consequences, including execution, imprisonment, or an imposed silence. Some of the well-known authors of this generation were Orixe, Ibiñagabeitia, Zaitegi, Guillermo Larrañaga, and Keperin Xemein.

The new generation of authors and postwar writers included José Luis Álvarez Enparantza "Txillardegi," Jon Mirande, Txomin Peillen, Federico Krutwig, and Salbatore Mitxelena. The postwar generation of the 1950s included a young group of writers that turned its back on the previous generation. Iñaki Aldekoa states that the new generation rejected the EAJ-PNV ideology and took a more radicalized stance against the Spanish regime that evolved into the establishment of the terrorist group, Euskadi ta Askatasuna, ETA (Basque Country and Freedom, 1959–2011). Among these radicalized writers, whose political and cultural views were evident through their works, were Krutwig (ideologist and militant of ETA), Mirande, "Txillardegi" (one of ETA's founding fathers), Juan San Martin, and Gabriel Aresti.[23] Little by little, the postwar generation of writers, the radical authors, began to leave *Euzko-Gogoa* aside and started to write in other magazines, including *Egan* (Flying) and *Jakin* (Knowledge). Both magazines were seen as more "current." Olaziregi states that the postwar generation of authors shared common characteristics: "Basque was not their mother tongue, they were sometimes agnostic, they held diverse political positions, and above all, they were distant from the traditional Basque nationalism of the EAJ-PNV."[24] The passing of the torch between the two generations was not a simple transition. One of the great debates was about what type of literary Basque should be used in *Euzko-Gogoa*. The inability to agree on one type of literary Basque among the various dialects formed an irreparable gap between the prewar and postwar generations. This linguistic dispute greatly affected the evolution of *Euzko-Gogoa*. In a letter sent from Zaitegi to Ibiñagabeitia in 1953, the discrepancies between the different generations regarding the standardization of the Basque language are evident: "I think Krutwig's [linguistic] pathway is getting worse. Orixe is getting more and more purist, as he states that the Basque language has a rich quarry that is still full. Of course! What a fool!"[25] Txillardegi argues that although it seems like a fairy tale today, the struggle for a unified Basque language was a reality, because the intentions of the new postwar generation were too novel for the narrow cultural Basque world. For the prewar writers, the fundamental criterion of the Basque language was the purity and rhetoric of the language rather than the message.[26]

Olaziregi states (2017, 149) that there were hardly any publications in Basque during these conflictive times in the Southern Basque Country. The exceptions were the novel *Loretxo* (Flower, 1937), written by Domingo Arruti, and *Uztaro* (Harvest Time, 1937), written by Tomas Agirre "Barrensoro." *Loretxo* was published as a series in the Basque newspaper, *Eguna* (Day, 1937), which was based in Bilbao and which published a total of 139 issues. After these publications, almost ten years of silence followed until the next publication which took place in exile—a direct result of Franco's policy of Basque cultural repression. As Torrealdai asserts, it took twenty years for Basque literature to recover from the wounds of the war (1993, xiv). Salbatore Mitxelena's *Arantzazu euskal sinismenaren poema* (Arantzazu, The Poem of the Basque Belief) was published in 1949. One year later, Jon Etxaide's *Alos-Torrea* (The Tower of Alos) and Orixe's *Euskaldunak* (The Basques) were also published. Both texts are similar to the costumbrista literature that prevailed until the arrival of the first modern Basque novel in 1957, *Leturiaren egunkari ezkutua* (Leturia's Secret Diary), written by José Luis Álvarez Enparantza "Txillardegi."

Txillardegi's novel became a milestone in Basque literary history. This book became the pathway for modern Basque literature. Nevertheless, *Leturiaren egunkari ezkutua* didn't bring heterogeneity to the Basque literary field, since the costumbrista novels were still strong. Koldo Mitxelena argues that the appeal of the costumbrista novel is in its crepuscular tone and in its nostalgia.[27] In fact, these novels represented a static world. That is, time passes physically, the characters age, but time is still psychological, because it is a time that does not evolve. The main Basque costumbrista author was the priest Txomin Agirre (1865–1920) and one of the best Basque writers. Ana Toledo (1989, 643) argues that no transformation in its settings takes place in Agirre's novels; the characters of this steady world maintain a Basque identity with no variations, connected to the rural world. On the other hand, Txillardegi's novel contributed to Basque literature by bringing a new sensibility to Basque novels, with a new scale of values and urban landscapes.

The tension and differences between the prewar and the postwar writers reflected a divided intellectual community, which eventually shaped a united imagined community. In fact, the postwar generation promoted a modernization of Basque literature. Txillardegi's novel *Leturiaren egunkari ezkutua* was the first step in the process of autonomization of Basque literature. For the postwar generation, the past no longer had a place in current Basque literature. As a result, the literary genre promoted by the prewar generation was perceived as anachronistic. These writers were living in the past, and they didn't recognize the present. In 1956, Jon Mirande wrote to Zaitegi: "I don't want to keep tasting the desired food of "fern-smell" [costumbrista novels]. Therefore, the postwar generation separated themselves from the previous generation."[28]

Nevertheless, *Euzko-Gogoa* embodied tenacity, resistance, and preservation during the worst cultural scenarios for the Basque language. Intxausti states that the magazine is the result of a group of humans silenced and scattered by Franco.[29] These authors came from a variety of professional backgrounds. Most of the writers who took part in the magazine were already active members of Basque culture during the Second Republic. Many of these writers lived during a time of war and felt the repercussions of the loss. However, the timing of the publication of the magazine allowed for the initial writings of a new generation of writers that were gaining a voice in the Basque Country. The magazine promoted the joint work between both generations and served as a bridge between the two. Most of the writers of the magazine were priests and Catholics, differing from most of the new generation of agnostic writers.

The End of *Euzko-Gogoa*

The end of *Euzko-Gogoa* was marked by new literary anxieties and desires of the generation of postwar writers. There was frustration and a sense that the new generation of writers didn't respect the efforts of the prewar generation to maintain and develop the Basque language. Bedita Larrakoetxea wrote to Zaitegi in 1958:[30] "Our great "Orixe" is not even mentioned among the best writers, and he is the best Basque writer alive."[31] While the prewar generation was originally optimistic in the belief that their footsteps would be followed, the newer writers tried to find their own path and original style of writing—ultimately distancing themselves from the old ways:[32]

> The magazine *Egan* (Flying) went dark in its last issue (5–6). When the magazine began to write entirely in Basque, "*Euzko-Gogoa*" gave it a good welcome; we also gave our approval to this magazine. *Egan* on the other hand, mentioned us poorly.[33]

For a magazine such as *Egan* and the new generation of writers, *Euzko-Gogoa* represented a continuation of prewar times and culture. Koldo Mitxelena wrote in the 1956 issue (5–6) an article in *Egan* in which he criticized the quixotic madness of Zaitegi and wrote with irony about the quality of his magazine:

> "The only Basque magazine" and also the "king among Basque magazines"—in the kingdom of the blind the one-eyed man is king—that is, "Euzko-Gogoa" . . . I am afraid that because he thinks that he is breaking the shadows of big a monster he is truly tilting at windmills."[34]

In the new reality of the Basque Country in the mid 1950s, Basque cities became the new cultural arena. Spain left behind its international ostracism, and its commercial ties were reinforced with the Western world. Aldekoa states that the moral beliefs of literary costumbrismo lost strength in the face of an aggressive character immersed in a new psychological, philosophical, and social reality laid before a new generation.[35] In other words, *Euzko-Gogoa* became obsolete with its old views and mentalities. According to Aldekoa, the change that began in the mid 1950s was carried out in the 1960s with the replacement of the prewar generation; the testimony went from the old to the young, updating old perspectives. The moral values of the traditional world evolved through religious, political, and social horizons without interruption (2015, 51).

This difference in opinion between the two generations of writers would create a difficult situation for the future of the magazine. Although it was intended to be an open-minded magazine, it was not received as such among the postwar generation. During the second stage of the magazine, in the Northern Basque Country, the Basque cultural reality changed, and new cultural platforms appeared, including the magazines *Jakin* (Knowledge) and *Egan* (Flying). Many writers turned their backs on Zaitegi at the end of *Euzko-Gogoa*'s existence because the previously imagined community did not reflect the new Basque reality. In fact, they created an anachronistic Basque nation. The idea of nation as apart from the language was rooted in the pillars of the preindustrial-prewar Basque world.

Despite *Euzko-Gogoa*'s global reach, the magazine had a very limited number of readers, which was a dilemma for the magazine from its inception. Zaitegi's school and other supporting institutions couldn't provide enough financial assistance. Without subscribers, the magazine couldn't have a future. During its time in Guatemala, 500 magazines were printed per issue, despite having only 339 subscribers. Also, as Velez de Mendizabal points out, 108 of the subscribers did not pay.[36] During its years in Biarritz, the number of subscribers increased to 874, and 1,000 magazines were printed per issue. However, according to Iztueta, many of the issues got lost along the way (2003a, 154). Zaitegi demonstrated concern with the survival of the magazine throughout its existence, explicitly in the issue (7–8) published in 1954:[37]

> "We are in our second year and there are people who didn't pay us for last year's subscription nor for this year. Don't believe that the magazine is rich. We need the help of all of you. Please send us the $10 subscription; those who can't, send us what you have. We need the effort of all of us to spread, enrich, and maintain the Basque language. Does our call have any answer from the Basque community?"[38]

Zaitegi would relocate to the Southern Basque Country because he thought that he would find a better home there for himself and the magazine. Most subscribers were from the Basque Country, and publishing there was seen as more conducive to distribution. Jon Diaz described the subscriber demographics as such: in the Basque Country (Hegoalde and Iparralde) 180, in Spain 10, Europe 41, and in America 108, for a total of 339 subscribers.[39] When Zaitegi moved to Biarritz, however, the situation didn't improve. Subscribers' lack of payments continued to dog the magazine.

The magazine not only had difficulties with the number of subscribers, but also with several economic issues because of Zaitegi's poor fiscal management. *Euzko-Gogoa* was Zaitegi's individual project. Since it wasn't directly affiliated with the Basque Nationalist Party, it did not receive Basque government grants, aside from the subscription of Agirre, the Basque president in exile.

To overcome the economic difficulties presented during Zaitegi's five years of publishing in Guatemala, he returned to the Southern Basque Country in 1955. Zaitegi's decision was driven by economics, personal reasons, and an effort to take advantage of a change in Franco's control over the Southern Basque Country.

Because of the political situation, Zaitegi made sure that he could enter Basque soil without any problems. Curiously, the regime didn't have anything against Zaitegi, but it did have issues with the magazine. During those years, the Basque language and Basque issues were an implicit political statement. As Joxe Azurmendi argues, the Basque language and Basque topics were taboo.[40] At this time, there was a subtle aperture on the part of the Franco regime that allowed the Basque culture to have a small presence in society. Olaziregi has explained that during those years several milestone magazines were published: *Jakin* (Knowledge) (1956), *Karmel* (Carmelite) (1950), and *Anaitasuna* (Brotherhood) (1953), which would provide an important cultural stage from which to launch a renewal of Basque cultural life.[41] With a glimmer of hope in a changing situation, Zaitegi felt it might allow him to continue his efforts closer to both subscribers and family.

Having been abroad for thirty years, homesickness was also a major factor behind his decision to return. In the last issue of *Euzko-Gogoa* published in Guatemala, the motivations behind Zaitegi's decision to leave the country were explained:[42]

> The director of the magazine has decided to repatriate and take the magazine to the nest of our ancestors. It is necessary. We can't deny our director's desire to return home; almost thirty years, the best years of his youth, have passed in exile fighting for the Basque language. He has his mother there, his relatives, and the Basque land waiting for him. And above all, there is our language, our old Basque, asking for warmth, love, and help. And we are sure that our director will continue working by giving warmth, love, and help to the Basque language.[43]

While the Southern Basque Country evolved and Basque identity adjusted to Franco's Spain, the imagined community created by *Euzko-Gogoa* was incongruent with the "real" Basque Country. In other words, the Basque community in the context of the political and cultural identity of the Southern Basque Country and the nation that Zaitegi had created were not the same. The optimistic ideas that Zaitegi had at the beginning of his Basque journey in exile were soon dissolved. Ironically, the new geographical scenario didn't work for the magazine. The identity and circumstances in the Basque Country had changed during his time in exile. *Euzko-Gogoa* found in Guatemala the perfect environment to develop. The sociopolitical, cultural, and economic situation during the "ten years of Guatemalan spring" allowed for an ideal milieu for Basque cultural cultivation.

The Return of Zaitegi and How *Euzko-Gogoa* Struggled to Find Its Place in the "New" Basque Context

When Zaitegi moved to the Southern Basque Country, he found a sociopolitical, cultural, and economic situation that wasn't the most favorable for the development of his project. The later 1950s marked a turning point with new horizons for Basque culture, politics, and religion that would drastically affect the magazine. In the Basque cultural arena, Zaitegi's enthusiasm toward Basque language and literature was greeted with hesitation and concern. Iztueta states that for most readers in the Basque Country, the cultural aspirations of Zaitegi were a trifle, and they turned a deaf ear (2003a, 154). Iztueta argues that Basque intellectuals were afraid that *Euzko-Gogoa* or Zaitegi could jeopardize their "privileges."

Pako Sudupe argues that Basque intellectuals and institutions did not want to take a risk and lose their ability to publish.[44] In that regard, Torrealdai analyzed the situation of the Basque language and the primary motives behind the Spanish regime's "approach" to Basque culture. He compiles the reasons why and how the magazine *Egan* (Flying) was created and was able to publish in the Southern Basque Country (1999, 62):

> The spiritual purpose pursued by the intended publication is to collect and channel, within the patriotic norms of the Society, the intellectual youth of the three provinces of the Basque Country, providing them with a platform for their activities. We also projected that some of their pages would be written in Basque—short stories and poetry—, a pure Basque, without arbitrary, experimental neologisms, precisely to try to undermine what the separatists did in this regard and not to leave this trump card in the hands of the enemies on the other side of the Pyrenees. The French Basques in close collaboration with the political emigrants have started an intense campaign in favor of Basque studies and we believe it prudent that they should not have exclusive rights both because of the deviation they could introduce to the very nature of the studies and because of what this could entail in and of itself.[45]

Unlike magazines such as *Egan* (Flying) and others, *Euzko-Gogoa* was considered a separatist element by the Spanish regime. To be able to publish the magazine in the Basque Country, the Francoist authorities demanded two unshakable conditions of Zaitegi, which Velez de Mendizabal recounts. First, Zaitegi was compelled to change the name of the magazine because it was too "Sabinian" (following the teachings of Sabino Arana). The second condition required Spanish translations of all the texts to be approved before publication.[46] Although Zaitegi tried to find support in the Basque intellectual community and institutions, his efforts failed. Seeing that Basque intellectuals and institutions were giving him the runaround, he tried other avenues. In the archives of Euskaltzaindia (The Royal Academy of the Basque Language), letters sent by Zaitegi during his time in the Southern Basque Country to Pablo Gurpide, the bishop of Bilbao, and to José Ibáñez Martín, the state president of the Superior Council of Scientific Research, demonstrate Zaitegi's efforts to promote his project. He also kept correspondence with the Spanish linguist Antonio Tovar, professor at the University of Salamanca, and the founder of the first Basque Language and Literature professorship in a Spanish university. Tovar was also a person close to Franco's regime who could help him with the publication of the magazine. In these letters, Zaitegi explains the nature of the magazine, presenting it as "nonpolitical" but religious, intellectual, and "homogeneous" (a white lie):[47]

> The magazine would be a Catholic intellectual type that would develop poetic, literary, philosophical, scriptural, theological, labor, historical, linguistic, musical, ascetical and pastoral topics, following pontifical norms and criteria clearly ecclesiastical and evangelical.[48]

In addition, Zaitegi highlighted the fact that politics didn't have a place in *Euzko-Gogoa*.[49] "Political questions of all kinds are prohibited in the magazine."[50] He also described the main topics that were discussed and analyzed in the magazine, as well as the profile of the writers:[51] "Those who have collaborated are outstanding members of Religious Orders and Congregations such as Jesuits, Passionists, Sacred Heartists, secular priests and laymen of renown religiousness and distinguished Catholic judgment."[52] He failed to mention the heterogeneity of the writers, and their different political beliefs and ideas. Zaitegi tried to blur the lines about the real identity of the magazine to pass the censorship. Zaitegi's only way to publish the magazine in the Southern Basque Country was by alienating himself and the identity of *Euzko-Gogoa* to appear more suitable to the Spanish regime. In the reality of the Southern Basque Country, defined by Franco's dictatorship, *Euzko-Gogoa* couldn't find a space.

Although the atmosphere wasn't the best or most welcoming for the magazine, Zaitegi didn't give up and decided to finance it with money he brought from Guatemala. As Velez de Mendizabal states, Zaitegi came from Guatemala with sixty thousand dollars and all his willpower.[53] Zaitegi was the kind of person who had faced adversity before. As his favorite proverb states, "gogorik denean aldaparik ez" [when you want to do something, there is no hill.] Seeing that it was impossible to publish the magazine in the Southern Basque Country, in the summer of 1956, he moved to Biarritz in the Northern Basque Country. In a letter sent by Zaitegi to Ibiñagabeitia in 1957 from Biarritz,[54] Zaitegi mentioned the frustrations he was facing in publishing the magazine in the Northern Basque Country: "I feel so alone, I am tired of most Basque writers. I came with the best of intentions, but I was barked at by the dogs I least expected."[55] One could assume that when Zaitegi moved to the Basque Country, it would be easier for him to develop *Euzko-Gogoa*, as it would be closer to the readers, since most of the subscribers and the writers were located there. However, it was not so: the gap *Euzko-Gogoa* faced was not just physical, but also cultural. Its content did not *reflect/speak to* the community of those times.

In the final years of the 1950s, many historical events occurred that changed the course of the Basque Country and therefore the future of *Euzko-Gogoa*. In 1959, the face of Basque nationalism changed with the founding of the armed group ETA Euskadi ta Askatasuna [Basque Country and Freedom]. Santiago De Pablo et al. (1999, 382) described this event in the following way: "The generational break that led to the appearance of ETA in 1959 was not only a new split, but the greatest transformation throughout the history of Basque nationalism."[56] ETA was the representation of the intransigence of a younger generation of nationalists. In fact, some of the new generation of writers for *Euzko-Gogoa* became members of ETA.[57]

Leyre Arrieta states (2015a, 52) that ETA's initial actions were limited to propagandistic work and cultural events for the promotion of the Basque language and culture. The Basque government was going through a massive internal crisis, and the Basque language wasn't its biggest concern. So, it was the leftist nationalists who took responsibility for safeguarding Basque culture through violent means. With this new approach toward the salvation of the Basque culture, some of the biggest cultural promoters, such as the writer Nikolas Ormaetxea "Orixe," were replaced, and the Basque language became more associated with the leftist nationalist movement. Txillardegi states that during that time, it was mostly the *ezker abertzalea* (the leftist nationalists) who were responsible for the Renaissance of Basque culture.[58]

Even though *Euzko-Gogoa* was at times critical of the EAJ-PNV, there was still a good relationship among some of the members. As previously stated, Zaitegi and Agirre, the Basque president in exile, had a long lasting and positive friendship. The death of Agirre in 1960 was a total shock for the Basque communities all over the world. With Agirre's death, Zaitegi's disillusionment with Basque culture and his dream only grew, and later that year the last issue of *Euzko-Gogoa* was published. Agirre's support was very important for Zaitegi, since the *lehendakari* always believed in Zaitegi's project and motivations. In a letter sent from Agirre to Zaitegi in 1951, it is possible to appreciate Agirre's admiration toward Zaitegi's work, *Euzko-Gogoa*:[59]

> Your magazine is getting better in every issue. The old Basque due to your influence is getting stronger and is getting ready for academia. You must keep doing this hard work, until our beloved motherland becomes free. This day, with the will of God, it will come.[60]

Following Agirre's death, Zaitegi unsuccessfully tried to find his place in the Basque intellectual community. Unfortunately, Zaitegi and *Euzko-Gogoa* were quite distant from the prevailing Basque atmosphere. Zaitegi wanted to find his niche, but despite his efforts he did not succeed. At the end of 1962, he decided to return to Guatemala. After ten more years in Guatemala, he returned to the Southern Basque Country in 1972 and passed away in 1979.

Euzko-Gogoa aspired to represent the dreams of those Jesuit students who found in Loyola the divine inspiration for the Basque language, culture, and nation. However, as the 1950s advanced, the great authors of the prewar period, many of them exiled, began to be dismissed by the younger generation of writers. The center of Basque culture was no longer in exile, but in the Southern Basque Country. Zaitegi was condemned to the margins of Basque culture. From one periphery (Guatemala) to an even more distant periphery (Biarritz), he was forced to isolate himself from an intellectual community that had closed its doors to him. Devastated and disappointed with the Basque community, he returned to Guatemala with nostalgia for a place where he had had better times and better memories. In fact, *Euzko-Gogoa* was rooted in Zaitegi's vision of a Basque nation or an ideal, imagined community. This imagined community could therefore be defined or demarcated and also romanticized for others, since Zaitegi was the director of the magazine, and his cultural consciousness and ideology had a strong presence in it. We can see an example of this in a letter sent by Ibiñagabeitia to Jon Mirande, in which Ibiñagabeitia explained that he changed certain elements of his work to make it more acceptable in Zaitegi's eyes:[61]

I sent to Guatemala your work about the Breton language among other works. I am telling you already that Zaitegi will love them. I loved them myself. I didn't send him the one about the prostitute for fear of what may happen. I also wrote to him about our poems. I think he will like our projects. I would like to publish your work before I move to the other side of the Atlantic. I am already working on that issue. Our language deserves all of our efforts. I also changed your words about 'Heidegger' and also what you said about Orixe; I think Zaitegi would appreciate it.[62]

Although *Euzko-Gogoa* was a space for cultural interaction, the truth is that the magazine was deeply rooted in Jokin Zaitegi's ideology and vision. In other words, *Euzko-Gogoa* was ultimately and uniquely Zaitegi's own project.

Notes

1. Ibid., 103.
2. Ibid., 104.
3. Ibid., 13.
4. Ibid., 73-81.
5. My translation.
6. Ibid., 7.
7. My translation.
8. Cardoza y Aragon, 1955, 9
9. Ibid., 102.
10. Ibid., 87. My translation.
11. *Euzko Irakastola Nagusia* (Superior Basque School) was the first public university in the Basque Country, created by the Basque government in 1936. The first course was launched on December 1, 1936, at an opening ceremony held at the School of Medicine of the Hospital of Basurto in Bilbao. In July 1937, the university had to close the doors because of the War of 1936 (Euskal Herriko hezkuntzaren historiarako dokumentazio basea http://www.ehu.eus/euskal-hezkuntza/euskara/).
12. Ibid., 59.
13. Ibid., 30.
14. My translation.
15. To know more about Orixe's life, see Iztueta, *Orixe saiogilea* and Azurmendi, *Zer dugu Orixeren alde*.
16. The parenthetical numbers refer to the magazine's issues.
17. See de Pablo et al., *100 Símbolos vascos: identidad, cultura, nacionalismo*.
18. Ibid., 92.
19. See Garde, *ELA a través de dos guerras (1936–1946)* (Through Two Wars: 1936–1946). Elorrieta, *Renovación sindical. Una aproximación a la trayectoria de ELA* (Social Renovation. An Approximation to the Trajectory of ELA) and Fusi,

Política obrera en el País Vasco 1880–1923 (Workers' Policy in the Basque Country 1880–1923) for an insightful analysis of this union.
20 Ibid., 131.
21 My translation.
22 My translation.
23 Ibid., 218–219.
24 Ibid.,152.
25 Jokin Zaitegi's letters 2.07.01 Gutuneria. KEH-0430-49936. Jokin Zaitegiren Funts Dokumentala. Euskaltzaindia. My translation.
26 Ibid., 45.
27 Ibid., 158.
28 February 24, 1956, in Andima Ibiñagabeitia's letters 2.07.01 Gutuneria. KEH-0430-49936. Jokin Zaitegiren Funts Dokumentala. Euskaltzaindia. My translation.
29 Ibid., 132.
30 February 6, 1958, in Andima Ibiñagabeitia's letters 2.07.01 Gutuneria. KEH-0430-49936. Jokin Zaitegiren Funts Dokumentala. Euskaltzaindia.
31 My translation.
32 *Euzko-Gogoa*, " 'Euskera' ta '*Euzko-Gogoa*'" 1956 (5-6), 1.
33 My translation.
34 My translation.
35 Ibid., 219.
36 Ibid., 112.
37 "Eup! Euzko-Gogoaren arpidedunei!" *Euzko-Gogoa* 27.
38 My translation.
39 Ibid., 178.
40 In Sudupe, 50eko hamarkadako euskal literatura. I, 24
41 Ibid., 152.
42 "Etxe-aldaketa," *Euzko-Gogoa* 1955 (5–12), 65
43 My translation.
44 "*Jakin* 1956–1961" 73.
45 My translation.
46 Ibid., 122.
47 August 13, 1955, in Jokin Zaitegi's letters. 2.07.01 Gutuneria. KEH-0433-50137. Jokin Zaitegiren Funts Dokumentala. Euskaltzaindia.
48 My translation.
49 August 13, 1955, in Jokin Zaitegi's letters. 2.07.01 Gutuneria. KEH-0433-50137. Jokin Zaitegiren Funts Dokumentala. Euskaltzaindia.
50 My translation.
51 August 13, 1955, in Jokin Zaitegi's letters. 2.07.01 Gutuneria. KEH-0433-50137. Jokin Zaitegiren Funts Dokumentala. Euskaltzaindia.
52 My translation.
53 Ibid., 117.
54 Letter to Andima Ibiñagabeitia. Miarritze, September 25, 1957. 2.02.1. AIB. KEH-0146. Box 006, File 242. Andima Ibiñagabeitiaren Funts Dokumentala.
55 My translation.

56 My translation.
57 See Zulaika, especially *Basque Violence,* for an insightful analysis of ETA.
58 Ibid., 23.
59 Agirre, José Antonio. Letter to Jokin Zaitegi. Paris, November 15, 1951. 2.07.01 Gutuneria. KEH-0427-49693. Jokin Zaitegiren Funts Dokumentala.
60 My translation.
61 Ibiñagabeitia, Andima. Letter to Jon Mirande. Paris, August 28, 1951. 2.02.4. AIB. KEH-0152. Box 012, File 001. Andima Ibiñagabeitiaren Funts Dokumentala.
62 My translation.

Chapter Four

The Imagined Community Created in *Euzko-Gogoa*

The cosmology of Basque exile has its own voice and was composed of a generation of Basque intellectuals who, although subjected to a painful historical experience, could sustain their cultural and political commitment and loyalty toward an ideal, the preservation of the Basque nation through its language. Jokin Zaitegi's poem "Erbestean aritza" (The Oak of Exile, 1952), showed the nostalgia and the homesickness of being in exile far away from the motherland:

> In the old, dark, blind forest far away from the Basque Country, / I found a strong oak. / I see myself in the oak / alone, strong, escaping from his motherland / This is what I am doing in exile: / the oak touched my heart. / The canopy of the tree is like a dove, / my white dream is spinning. / I took one of his branches / maybe trying to ease my misfortune. / I have my homeland inside my heart / in exile my wound was revived. / I shouldn't look at the oak, / to remember you, because I love you. / The Basque Country is always in my heart within me, / even if I live far away in exile.[1]

This chapter analyzes the imagined community and the nation that *Euzko-Gogoa* built in its ten years of existence. In fact, the primary focus of this research is to examine how the writers of *Euzko-Gogoa* came to imagine their nation. From its place in exile, the magazine gave the Basque community—both writers and readers—an enduring sense of "us," the Basques. After losing the War of 1936, many Basques who fought against the Francoist troops suffered the revenge of the victors. The violence of the winners revolved around the extermination of memory, identity, language, and history. Many Basques were forced to leave their homeland and move to other countries for fear of reprisals that could be taken by the authoritarian political regime established in Spain. *Euzko-Gogoa* was a platform that allowed the building of an imagined community that could be a reference for future Basque nation building.

Euzko-Gogoa became a "therapeutic" response against the Basque cultural defeat. A step toward the reconstruction of a nation, the magazine built throughout its pages an imagined community, a utopian nation, that was forbidden in the Basque Country. In fact, Benedict Anderson considers that nations are social constructs existing in the minds of their members, and that newspapers play a central role in creating and sustaining "an imagined community among a specific assemblage of fellow-readers."[2] Anderson envisioned newspaper readers conjuring such a community in their minds. In this regard, *Euzko-Gogoa* was a way to help overcome the trauma of the defeated Basque nation. It was a cultural instrument providing renewed hope for the annihilated Basque people and country.

Through its pages, *Euzko-Gogoa* built an imagined community that could be shared with its readers. In doing so, it achieved a collaboration for the reconstruction of the homeland, creating a common, collective sentiment about the Basque nation. To identify the nation, the idea, the feeling, and the voice that was built in the magazine, the different identity markers or pillars on which *Euzko-Gogoa* was built will be further addressed: language, religion, gender, and nation/politics. The construction of a nation requires a shared sense of national identity, built on elements that tie people together. This sentiment is evident in the magazine's first publication:[3]

> This magazine is for you, beloved Basque Country; we offer it to you because we have you in our deepest dreams; we, your honest and pure children, give you all of our efforts: we wish you your freedom. Those who want to be your dearest sons, beloved motherland, our God knows that we love you more than anything. We are ready to offer the red blood of our veins for you. Because we haven't forgotten what Arana stated: We for the Basque Country, and the Basque Country for God[4]

The magazine's writers were essential in establishing *Euzko-Gogoa*'s tone. They were a heterogeneous group of Basque authors, from different generations, realities, experiences, and ideologies, although most were patriots and *euskaltzales* (Basque language lovers). In the political sphere, the majority were Christian-Democrats and members of the EAJ-PNV (Basque Nationalist Party). The imagined community created in the magazine was built within the scope of the prewar generation, also known as Aitzol's generation (José Ariztimuño "Aitzol" Tolosa (Gipuzkoa), 1896 - Hernani (Gipuzkoa), 17.10.1936 was a Basque priest, writer, journalist, and politician) since almost all the writers were culturally active before the war. But above all, because it was Zaitegi's personal project, and he was part of that generation. Later, Nikolas Ormaetxea "Orixe" and Andima Ibiñagabeitia helped with the direction of the magazine; they were also from the prewar generation.

Basque Language

The Basque language played a crucial role in both the magazine's content and its mission of creating a Basque nation. From the start, the Basque language was a cornerstone of the magazine:[5] "We want to sustain, beautify and expand the Basque language each of us, as much as we can." *Euzko-Gogoa* wanted to demonstrate that Basque had the same strength, capacity, and beauty as any other language. They wanted to open new paths to the language and show its depth: "Ortarako orindik landu-gabe zauden gure alorretan ildo berriak urratzen asiak gera" [We opened new paths in areas that were not done before.] After the War of 1936, the Basque language was persecuted and repressed. The Spanish government harassed those who used the Basque language to the point that Basque people remained mute for fear of retaliation. Paul Preston claims (2003, 13) that Spain was polarized between "the privileged authentic Spain and the punished anti-Spain."[6] The Basque Country was on the "*anti-España*" side, forced into a cultural rupture with its roots and traditions. The extermination of a people's history, memory, and identity became a fact in areas across the Basque Country, especially in the provinces of Bizkaia and Gipuzkoa, which had been declared "traitors" by the victors.

THE FOUNDATION OF BASQUE NATION BUILDING WAS THE BASQUE LANGUAGE

For the magazine, the main pillar in the foundation of Basque nation building was the Basque language. The Basque language was what connected the country, the people, and their identity: "The Basque language is what makes us Basque; we don't want a Basque Country without Basque language."[7] Ngũgĩ wa Thiong'o and Frantz Fanon have mentioned the intrinsic power of language and people, and the devastating consequences of this rupture in people's identity. For Basque individuals, the inability to speak their language gave an impression that they were also unable to be themselves.

The Catholic patriotism promoted by EAJ-PNV was left behind, and the 1960s embraced "new" patriotic parameters. For the new generation, the Basque language became the sociopolitical and cultural cornerstone; in fact, as Aldekoa states, "political and cultural recognition appeared linked together as the first and last terms of a binomial."[8] However, this relationship between the Basque language and culture on the one hand and patriotism and politics on the other hand was already in evidence in *Euzko-Gogoa* in the 1950s. What appears to be something new of the postwar generation was already rooted by the prewar generation.

One of the strongest arguments of the magazine is that without the Basque language there is no Basque Country. The inherent union between the language and the nation was foundational for the magazine. This relationship began in the early nineteenth century with the loss of the *fueros* (the old Basque laws) and the beginning of the Basque literary renaissance in 1876. Olaziregi argues that when the *fueros* and their concomitant right were abolished in 1876, this same year marked the beginning of a more militant arena for Basque language and culture.[9]

Euzko-Gogoa continued the fight, initiated decades before the magazine's existence, for the survival of the Basque language. Because of the imposition of Spanish language and culture, there was a strong resistance to the possibility of losing the Basque language and identity. As we saw in chapter one, the scholars Frantz Fanon and Ngũgĩ wa Thiong'o argue that by adopting the language of the colonizer, the world of the colonizer is accepted. The suppression of one's language is the suppression of one's own identity and one's own world. Language is not only a means of communication but also a means of cultural expression. These Basque intellectuals used the platform of *Euzko-Gogoa* as a means of resistance to maintain their community.

The relationship between language and the identity of a people was strongly promoted in the pages of *Euzko-Gogoa*. Iztueta (2001, 83) states: "*Euzko-Gogoa* made a huge step in the language, taking the Basque language, as the main feature of popular identity; it was something new for Basque nationalism." The nation building that was promoted, founded upon the Basque language, showed a resistance to Spanish censorship.

In Franco's Spain, cultural plurality was forbidden. The writers of the magazine were concerned about the difficulties that the Basque language was facing, and out of opposition they wrote only in the Basque language. Zaitegi considered language the main key to the Basque people and their country's freedom and salvation:[10]

> *Euzko-Gogoa*, We only want to write in Basque, to get at the deepest heart of the Basque will: we lose the key to our freedom if we lose the Basque language; and the country that has lost its language has no place in the world, if it is lost, and it is no longer alive. An independent country will never be a servant of anyone. So, we have to get together in preparation for the day of our freedom.

The cultural repression carried out in Spain during the postwar period was of such magnitude that many Basque people tried to forget the Basque language to avoid possible reprisals. The writers of *Euzko-Gogoa* knew that it was punishable to speak Basque under these circumstances. However, they knew that it was necessary to keep its flame alive. They believed that the Basque language was the path forward for a civilization and that it transmitted wisdom and a way of life; it constituted a universe, a heritage, and a distinguishing mark. While in exile and through the Basque language, Zaitegi endeavored to achieve the forbidden freedom for the Basque Country, a freedom for a people who were subjugated at the mercy of the "Spanish Empire," a Spain that felt that the coexistence of more than one language would result in the failure of its own foundations. Implementing Spanish as the only language of culture was a unifying and civilizing function from the Francoist perspective. This belief is still strongly rooted in Spain. Luisa Elena Delgado (2014, 102) explained how the Spanish language became the "glue" for both its internal and external use of a promotional strategy of the country's image. *Euzko-Gogoa* resisted it to subvert "colonization."

Nevertheless, the rupture of the transmission of the Basque language between generations was becoming the norm in many Basque families. Some parents were afraid of the negative political and social repercussions that the Basque language could have on their children. This linguistic and cultural fracture between the two generations was dangerous; it could bring about the death of the language and the nation, as well as subjugation to the Spanish and French states, Zaitegi wrote:[11]

> However, the sons of our country, even if they are nationalist, put the Basque language aside and they speak in Spanish or in French. Their parents, nationalist, and their sons didn't hear Basque at home. Where does this plague come from? Where do the Spanish and French tendencies come from? The roots of this disease have to be cut off.

This linguistic break in transmission worried Zaitegi because the Basque nation's future depended on the next generation continuing to speak and share Basque. In this regard, the magazine criticized the lack of action on the part of certain Basque institutions that were too cowardly and too aware of Spanish state repercussions and were not setting an example for the people: "Your prudence is a vain and deadly habit; our craziness on the other hand, is the courage and vigor that will revitalize the Basque language."[12]

The lack of Basque institutional strength and their fear of commitment did not help the Basque language. The Spanish Second Republic in 1936 approved a statute of autonomy promoted by Basque president Agirre's government. This statute declared Basque as an official language. However, the military uprising ended Basque autonomy and its internal laws. The Basque language lost its support following the war and was no longer allowed. The truth was that the Spanish and the French languages were choking the Basque language: "The Romance languages have long been taking large spaces of our language."[13] Therefore, the magazine encouraged readers to work in favor of Basque. Gotzon Urrutia stated: "The Basque language will not die. Unless the Basques kill it; and we never will be the murderers of our language."[14] For the magazine, the Basque language was intrinsically connected with the country and with its people. That is why the magazine promoted artistic and cultural production in Basque as a strategic way to build a specific image of the country: culture as a cohesive element, a generator of union, and a tool for resistance.

If the Basque language wanted to survive, it had to have the support of different social classes. Federico Krutwig argues[15] that language is the most useful tool employed by humans; if the tool is not valid, it is no longer used. Therefore, it was one of the magazine's main priorities to the Basque language to find its place in both high society as well as in everyday life: "If everyone with a hat (high society members) speaks Basque, that will soon become its salvation."[16] Many upper-class people saw in the Basque language a "barbaric" language that was used only by rustic or country people. Torrealdai collects in *El libro negro del euskera* (The Black Book of the Basque Language) some of the most famous sentences of disdain and mockery written by writers and intellectuals of "educated languages" about the Basque language, which they described as "idioma bárbaro," "lenguaje grosero," and "algarabía" (barbaric language, rude language, and a noisy racket). These ideas about the inferiority of the Basque language date back to the eighteenth century. As Joseba Zulaika states (1988, 17), "With the ascendance of the Bourbon dynasty to Spanish thrones in the eighteenth century and the advent of a liberal regime in Madrid in the early nineteenth century, state centralism became the overriding national goal." The twentieth century brought the process of industrialization and modernization, and with it the idea that the Basque language could not encompass modern thought. In 1901, Miguel de Unamuno called for accepting the death of the Basque language, arguing its incapacity to be a language of the modern world.

The stigmatization of the Basque language did not only come from intellectuals of "cultured languages" but also from Basque intellectuals themselves. *Euzko-Gogoa* was critical toward Basque intellectuals who despite knowing the language, were using Spanish or French in their writings: "Intellectuals didn't like Basque, and they wrote in Spanish or French."[17] Disparaging the Basque language and stereotypes associated with it had to be discouraged. Basque had to be shown to be as valid as any other language as a vehicle for the spread of scientific and cultural communication. It was necessary to convince readers and intellectuals of the linguistic capacity of their language; otherwise Romance languages would monopolize the cultural field:[18]

> We want to welcome intellectuals. We are opening new paths for the Basque language. If we bring professors and students to our side, the Basque language will stay alive in its beauty and its grandeur.

Gotzon Urrutia argues that the Basque language was not just "a language for smalltalk in the kitchen."[19] The magazine was hoping to end the ostracism of the Basque language and bring it into everyday life and academia. Ibiñagabeitia wrote: "The Basque language is capable of explaining everything, even the darkest topics, in the hands of Basque language loyalists and nationalists."[20] Zaitegi and Ibiñagabeitia always demonstrated their concern about the future of the Basque language. They repeatedly insisted that Basque should be a language of educated people, not a language for just certain fields or used as mere folklore. Without writers and intellectuals using the Basque language as a medium, they feared the language and their country would lose its essence.

THROUGH THE BASQUE LANGUAGE TO A BASQUE UNIVERSITY
An additional proposal from *Euzko-Gogoa* was that a Basque university should be established. This university would continue to promote the use of Basque in different fields of study at the highest levels. In the last issue of 1957, the magazine analyzed the benefits that a Basque university could offer and tried to show the capabilities of the Basque language that could one day be used in a collegiate realm. As stated by Ernest Gellner, high culture with a unique shared language is key for nation building and creating a more modern society.[21] Although the political situation at this time would not allow for the creation of a university, these intellectuals saw the value of higher education.

The magazine showcased the linguistic sophistication of the Basque language in issue (9-12) through three dramatic texts: *Piloktete* (Philoctetes, 1957) by Sophocles, *Macbeth* (1957) by Shakespeare, and *Menditarrak* (Mountaineers, 1957) by Telésforo Monzón. As they discussed in the introduction, these works could have been written more simply, but the authors decided to translate them in a more rigorous and authentic way, despite knowing the difficulty that it would entail for the reader: "Those who only speak *common* Basque, even if they are members of the Basque Language Academy, are not going to be able to appreciate the beauty of these plays."[22] The difficulties that may have arisen in these readings indicated the necessity of having a Basque university; Norbert

Taur wrote: "Because the Basques don't have a Basque University, they can't properly learn their language, and therefore read in Basque."[23]

A Basque university was indispensable in bringing the Basque language to the highest level possible: "Our will must be materialized by the Basque language. Our fight will be decided by the Basque language: this is our biggest and most vivid desire."[24] Zaitegi was convinced that the recovery of the Basque language was linked to its use by the Basque intelligentsia. He believed that literate Basques should be the force for improving and developing the Basque language. That was the way to create a Basque university, placing Basque intellectuals and therefore any science in favor of the Basque language. The magazine presented themes that were relatively new for the Basque readers in the 1950s, including psychology, metaphysics, biology, botanic, music, esthetics, and philosophy. Ibiñagabeitia, Orixe, and especially Jon Mirande's works opened new avenues to the Basque language and to its linguistic capacities. These articles about various fields of knowledge were especially strong during the first period of the magazine.

Josu Chueca argues that the need and demand for a Basque university got stronger in the twentieth century (2000, 395). From that need, in 1918 Eusko Ikaskuntza (The Basque Studies Society) and Euskaltzaindia (The Royal Academy of Basque Language) were established. The Basque Public University, more specifically the College of Medicine, was created in October 1936 when the War of 1936 had already begun. Mikel Aizpurua in his article argues that although the loss of the war eliminated the university, it didn't extinguish its flame.[25] The 1950s with its social and economic changes led many Basque intellectuals to promote and expand higher education in the Basque language and create Basque language professorships or positions in various American universities including the Basque Studies program at the University of Nevada, Reno. Therefore, *Euzko-Gogoa*'s calls for a Basque university echoed the desires of its community.

"GIPUZKERA OSATUA:" THE LITERARY BASQUE LANGUAGE

Another strong focus of the magazine was highlighting the necessity of standardizing the Basque language. Zaitegi, among other writers of the magazine, made an important contribution to standardized Basque. *Euzko-Gogoa* created a space of empowerment, a network, and a voice for a standard Basque language. The magazine became a platform for the dissemination of and debate about the language: "If we want to strengthen our language, if we want it to be capable of literary expression, its unity is essential."[26] The magazine offered a forum in which to develop the discourse about standard Basque: "Basques and

Basque writers. Here is the most beautiful and highest thing to do: to organize and unify a complete and concrete Basque language for us and for our heirs."[27] The debate about the standardization of the Basque language that had begun decades before continued in the magazine and was echoed in other platforms during the 1960s, culminating in 1968 when *euskara batua* (standard Basque) was consolidated and Euzkaltzaindia conferred its support and protection.

In their writings, Zaitegi and Ibiñagabeitia promoted Azkue's *gipuzkera osatua* (enhanced Gipuzkoan), a dialect of Basque very similar to the one that was accepted in 1968. Numerous questions and different opinions about the use of Basque and its standardization were shared and discussed through *Euzko-Gogoa*'s pages. Some of them were: *erderakadak* (the use of foreign words), neologisms, *gipuzkera osatua* (enhanced Gipuzkoan), *lapurtera klasikoa* (literary Labourdian), and *mordollokeriak* (jargon). The writers found in the magazine a privileged site for the development of all these topics related to the establishment and normalization of *euskara batua* (standard Basque). Although the directors of the magazine strongly supported *gipuzkera osatua* (enhanced Gipuzkoan) as a literary variety, other opinions also found their place in *Euzko-Gogoa*.

One of the main debates in the magazine was about which literary language should be used. This discussion evolved into an irreparable disagreement between the prewar and postwar generations. The Basque language didn't have a literary standard. It was seen as essential to choose one and establish an institutional platform to teach it. Since there wasn't a Basque university or language institute, *Euzko-Gogoa* took on the responsibility of attempting to create and promote a standardized Basque.[28]

The dispute over which standardized Basque would be the ideal one was between enhanced Gipuzkoan and literary Labourdian. The prewar generation of writers primarily promoted enhanced Gipuzkoan, and young writers of the postwar generation favored literary Labourdian. Orixe penned an article suggesting Krutwig, a writer of the postwar generation, write in enhanced Gipuzkoan:[29]

> You use labourdian Basque. You are not the first one to use it. In Euskaltzaindia (The Royal Academy of Basque Language) previously, some of us were in favor of it until Azkue came out with his enhanced Gipuzkoan. We will see if you are better than we are.

In articles about the correct use of the Basque language, Orixe and Martin Oiartzabal determined themselves to be "moderate purists" because they were not opposed in principle to neologisms.[30] From their point of view, they had to be seen as helpful resources who enriched the Basque language. They agreed on the necessity of adaptation and appropriation because the educated/cultured languages must accept these terms to evolve and become global. Nevertheless, although Orixe didn't like jargon, he argued that each one should know where the limits are, it was in the writer's hand what type of Basque used at the end.[31] The debate about Basque reflected a divided opinion among the writers. However, if the Basque language were to survive, all the writers had to work together. Juan San Martin argued in the article "Eritzi baten eritzia" (Opinion about an Opinion, 1957)[32] that, even if their ideas were different, at least they should respect them, and they should try to avoid polarization by working toward the same goal:

> Those who are working, in pure Basque or impure Basque (because both are necessary, each one in their own measure), we should help each other and be happy, and they should be better acknowledged, and never without knowing the purpose of the writer.

Despite their differences, all the writers of the magazine agreed that it was necessary to normalize the Basque language for literature. For its betterment, the language needed to be nourished in different ways to achieve its highest level.

Another debate was the level of difficulty that should be used in writings. Should Basque be written for intellectuals. As we saw before, José Ariztimuño "Aitzol" and José María Agirre "Xabier Lizardi" had the same dilemma. Aitzol initially promoted an intellectual Basque, although he later retracted his comment and expressed his support for everyday Basque. Zaitegi, Orixe, and Keperin Xemein argued that the solution could be to keep both types of language. One Basque for people's everyday life, and another for intellectual discourse, administration, and education, among others: "Sometimes we have to write in a language that people can't understand. But don't worry, doesn't this same thing happen in every language?"[33]

Other writers and some Basque institutions condemned the use of a high-level or "difficult" Basque by some of the magazine's writers. Orixe wrote an article reporting the criticism and scorn he suffered because of his "difficult" Basque. He also added: "The difficult Basque that we use is not going to kill the popular Basque. The popular Basque that you want will also not prevent the death of the Basque language."[34] For Orixe, the level of Basque used wasn't the debate; for him the simple fact of writing in Basque would allow the language to survive. Zaitegi added that it wasn't the Basque language that was difficult, but rather the topics. He believed that sometimes it was necessary to write at a higher level to explain a topic, even though some individuals wouldn't comprehend: "Sometimes the difficulty of the language is due to the topics. The topics that we use in the magazine would be difficult to understand in any language. Our topics are for intellectuals."[35] He promoted respect for the different types of Basques, which depended greatly on the purpose of the text, because all the forms had their own use in different fields of society.

Zaitegi wrote a letter to Ibiñagabeitia in 1957 bemoaning the lack of communication with Euskaltzaindia and the power that Koldo Mitxelena and Antonio Arrue had in their hands: "What is ordered by Mitxelena and Arrue is what is done in Euskaltzaindia. They increased the number of corresponding members of the academy; I believe that they are acting out of selfishness."[36] Mitxelena became the main point of reference for the standardization of the Basque language. As Zuazo (2005, 157) states, Euskaltzaindia left in Mitxelena's hand the standardization of the Basque language. Postwar generation writers such as Txillardegi and Gabriel Aresti supported Mitxelena's standard Basque.

TRANSLATIONS TO SHOW THE CAPACITY OF THE BASQUE LANGUAGE
Another feat of the magazine was the use of translation to show the capacity of the Basque language. Moreover, the works chosen by the editors and authors play an important role in understanding the subliminal messaging of nation building and the aspirations of the magazine. With an immense number of works from which to choose to translate, the purpose of analyzing the translations is to determine the rationale for choosing the selected texts and their importance.

Iztueta affirms "the editors of *Euzko-Gogoa* are convinced that translations are necessary to put the Basque language in the cultural pathway."[37] Most of the works were translated from the original language and became a linguistic tool to show the grammatical, morphosyntactic, syntactical, vocabulary, capacity of the language in *Euzko-Gogoa*. In fact, 13.5 percent of the articles of the magazine were translations.

Translations of authors of the Western literary canon, such as Aeschylus, Sophocles, Cicero, Virgil, Shakespeare, Goethe, Kafka, and the paradigmatic *poètes maudits* Baudelaire and Verlaine were part of the magazine's corpus. The works of various Nobel Prize winners were also translated: Sully Prudhomme 1839, Henryk Sienkiewicz 1846, Jacinto Benavente 1866, Juan Ramón Jiménez 1881, Gabriela Mistral 1889, and Selma Lagerlöf 1909. Also, literature by authors writing in minority languages were transcribed into Basque: Miquel Costa i Llobera, León Jasson, and Joan Maragall, among others. The works of the selected writers were chosen to be translated, I believe, because *Euzko-Gogoa*'s editors wanted to provide a systematic explanation of why Basque culture should appeal to a particular group of people, in which they could exhibit the central values of their purpose, to structure the self-image of the Basque culture.

The late Romantic German poets had a strong presence in the first period of the magazine. The works of authors such as Ludwig Uhland, Joseph Freiherr von Eichendorff, Christian Johann Heinrich Heine, Baron Detlev von Liliencron, and Eduard Friedrich Mörike were translated into Basque. The works of the poets Uhland and Heine were translated more than once. Mirande translated several of Uhland's poems, including *Ba-nin adiskide bat* (I Had a Comrade, 1950), a funeral march of the German armed forces.

Joxe Azurmendi (1978, 51) states that Mirande showed himself to be in favor of the German Nazis when he argued that "France is the enemy of Basques and Germans, are the enemy of our enemy."[38] Mirande, inspired by Nazi ideology, argued that for the resurrection of the Basque Country there had to be strength and blood. He saw in French democracy and liberalism the loss of small nations. Joxe Azurmendi claims that Mirande believed in the spirit of Old Europe: "A free spirit, bourgeois, individualist, aristocratic, proud knight, tough."[39] In my opinion, Mirande sees in this poem the spirit he would like to see in the Basque Country, a spirit willing to fight for its freedom and the salvation of its culture. This mentality was shared among other contributors of *Euzko-Gogoa* and can be seen as well in the future generations of the Basque Country, who would contribute to the eventual formation of ETA.

Zaitegi translated Heine's *Nere atsekabe aundi* (Out of my great unrest, 1951) and Anbrozio Zaratain translated *Balekiye* (And if they knew it, the blooms, the little ones, 1950). Because of his Jewish origin and his political position, Heine, for example, was constantly excluded and harassed until he finally left Germany and went into exile. Zaitegi was an outcast of the Jesuit order and an outcast in the Basque intellectual community, resulting in his various exiles.

Another commonly translated author was Johann Wolfgang von Goethe, one of the central figures of the Romantic movement in Europe. Romanticism believed in the world of ideals, creating a unique world between dream and imagination. *Euzko-Gogoa* acquired some ideas from Romanticism, especially when it decided to create its own imagined community. Romantic authors preach the singularity of the individual and the nation. Therefore, romantic authors had great weight in the magazine, since they promoted the unique identity of the individual and the nation, the desired goal of the Basque community both at home and abroad.

Mirande also translated Edgar Allan Poe's *Ixiltze; Alegia* ("Siope/Silence: A Fable," 1951), *Bela* ("The Raven," 1950), and *Amontillado upela* ("The Cask of Amontillado," 1952) and Franz Kafka's *Legearen aitzinean* ("Before the Law,"

1954). Mirande's translations were a new element for Basque literature since they dealt with subjects that had not been part of the Basque literary scene before. However, it is interesting to see how *Euzko-Gogoa*, often criticized as "too traditional," dedicated space to the fantastic world of Mirande. Otaegi mentions that the works of Poe and Kafka show the dark side of human's identity, the perverse, and the violent (2000, 21). Mirande criticized and broke away from the stereotype of the honest and Christian Basque and, through his translations, favored violence, paganism, and darkness. In this regard, Azurmendi holds that "Jon Mirande was the precursor and one of the strongest promoters of a new movement. It can be said that he was the forerunner of ETA in many ways."[40] The desires of Mirande's imagined community may have differed greatly from those of various contributors to *Euzko-Gogoa*, but the magazine allowed a platform for debate. Despite differing opinions, they shared the common goal of having a free Basque Country and making the language a contributor to the nation.

Following the winds of change, the poet Gabriel Aresti brought new pathways to Basque literature. When he was in his twenties, he contributed to *Euzko-Gogoa* with his translations of Charles Baudelaire's *Gauontzak* ("The Owls," 1954) and Paul Verlaine's *Udazken-kantuak* ("Autumn Song," 1954). These authors were important in the modernization of French poetry, a poetry that showed the inner city and urbanization in a different context than before. For Aresti, a person brought up in a city environment far from the often-romanticized Basque farming communities, his translations reflected a change of demographics and the urbanization of the Basque Country. These works were signs of change ahead and the development of a new reality with a new generation. Again, *Euzko-Gogoa* published a variety of opinions, which also allowed for a transition and a bridge between generations of authors.

The works of Greco-Latin authors were also often translated in the magazine. Iztueta states that "they go to the roots of the tradition to find the esthetics."[41] The classical works of literature are the key to understanding humanity, essential knowledge, and cultural heritage. Having a foundational scope of literature would also serve as an important tool for a future Basque university. In the Western canon, Shakespeare was one of the most translated authors in the magazine. *King Lear* was translated twice by two different writers: Eladi Larrañaga in 1951 *Lear erregea* and Bedita Larrakoetxea in 1958 *Lear Errege*. Other translated works of Shakespeare were *Neguko ipuia* (Winter's Tale, 1950), *William Shakespeare LXVI'garren amalaukoa* (LXVI. Sonnet, 1954), *CIXgarren sonetua* (CIX. Sonnet,1954), *Macbeth* (Macbeth, 1957), and *Ekatxa* (The Tempest, 1959). The ability to translate timeless works of such global fame for their beauty and complexity proved that the Basque language was capable even of Shakespearian poetry.

Josu Insausti and Luis Mari Mujika translated children's and young adult literature. This was quite unusual because most readers of the magazine were not exactly young. Nevertheless, I think it helped to promote the use of the Basque language in all subjects and at all levels: at the university, in secondary schools, and in primary schools. *Euzko-Gogoa* believed that the future of the Basque language was in the youth: "Educated youth can do many and great things; they will be the future."[42] Insausti translated some of the short stories in the collection, *My Name is Aram* (1954–1955), written by Armenian American writer William Saroyan. The stories depict Aram Garoghlanian, an Armenian American child from Fresno, California, as the main character. In the stories, topics consist of the immigrant experience, family, honesty, and love. Work of Italian children's writer Carlo Collodi was also translated. Mujika adapted *The Adventures of Pinocchio* (1959) into the Basque language. Also, in this group of translations for youth was *One Thousand and One Nights* (1956–1958), translated by Guillermo Larrañaga. What is most interesting is the moral of the story and how it is the richness of the protagonist's culture that allows the character to survive. An underlying message to Basque youth and the magazine's readers is that with the promotion and maintenance of language and culture, both an individual and their country can survive what may have appeared to be an imminent death. Although the magazine's potential readers were older, the publication promoted canonical advanced literature for youth.

Written Basque was late to arrive; the first Basque book was not published until the sixteenth century. Xabier Etxaniz states that it was not until the nineteenth century that children's literature found its place. In 1804, Bixenta Mogel, the first significant female Basque writer, published the first literary-didactic book for children titled *Ipui Onac* (Good Stories); it was a translation of Aesop's fifty fables. She also created the foundation for children's literature (Etxaniz 26). The translations show an open political approach far from religion or folklore. As Seve Calleja explains, from 1920 to 1930, most of children's literature was focused on developing Sabino Arana's nationalist ideology and promoting "ereduzko umea" [model children] (93), such as the book *Xabiertxo* written in 1925 by Ixaka Lopez-Mendizabal. After the War of 1936, because of the strict censorship, there were hardly any publications. In 1950, thanks to a small decrease in censorship, publication of children's literature in the Southern Basque Country increased. However, the recurrent topics continued to be religion, morality, folklore, legends, and education: *Kristau-ikasbidea bertsotan* (Christian Doctrine in Verse, 1950), *Kartak nola idatzi euskaraz?* (How to write letters in Basque? 1950) written by Nemesio Etxaniz, and Antonio Sorrain's *Santa Maria Goretti* (Saint Mary Goretti, 1950). In 1951, two catechisms in two different dialects were published. Calleja states that the translation *Noni eta Mani* (Noni and Mani, 1952) was an important step for the genre of children's literature since it was an adventure book (101). However, I am surprised to see that the translations published in *Euzko-Gogoa* did not have more of an impact on Basque children's literature since they were high-quality canonical works and they promoted new topics. Nevertheless, it was only in the 1960s when children's literature in the Basque language changed its patterns and took another path, much more dynamic than the previous one.

Spanish authors and literature were also adapted in *Euzko-Gogoa*. They translated the works of two winners of the Nobel Prize in Literature: Jacinto Benavente and Juan Ramón Jiménez. They also translated the works of Basque writers Pío Baroja, Arturo Campión, and José Miguel Barandiaran. Baroja was a Basque writer of the so-called Generation of '98. Campión was a Basque nationalist, writer, and linguist, and one of the founders of Euskaltzaindia (Royal Academy of the Basque Language) in 1918.

The translated works of Campión, *Erraondoko azken danbolinteroa* (The Last Drummer of Erraondo, 1952, 1955), *Itzaltzu'ko koblaria* (The Bard of Itzaltzu, 1954), and *Izkuntza eta abenda* (Language and Race, 1959) made various statements in the magazine about many realities of the Basque Country. There is a sense of nostalgia from the writer for a "primitive" Basque Country, one far from the impacts of globalization and external forces. In the story *Erraondoko azken danbolinteroa*, Campión criticizes the process of Hispanization of Navarrese rural life. The story's protagonist is a Navarrese shepherd, Pedro Fermin Izko, who, after decades of work in a farm in the Argentinean Pampas, decides to return to his hometown in Navarre and does not recognize his native town. In this regard, Campión criticizes the depersonalization or loss of Navarrese identity. He highlights the importance of roots and shows the reality of exiled people and their difficulties upon returning to a country that has evolved without their presence. It is possible to observe nostalgia, the foundation of literary costumbrismo (the static and rural world), and the impossible return of immigrants to their roots since the motherland has changed and they do not fit into it anymore.

The text *Itzaltzu'ko koblaria* (The Bard of Itzaltzu) is based on the life of Gartxot, a medieval Basque bard. Gartxot is a folkloric character who fought against the Christianization of the Basque Country. The character strives to maintain his culture and avoid the conquering of his spirit. Guillermo Larrañaga translated *Izkuntza eta abenda* (Language and Race) and wrote of it: "It has been more than fifty years since this work appeared. Since then time has passed; however, these truths are still prominent" (24). What Campión condemned a half a century before—the potential death of the Basque language because of the unwillingness of the Basques to keep it alive—was still a main concern in *Euzko-Gogoa*. Campión uses these folkloric characters as a reference to stand against the colonization and execution of the culture. These publications brought us the legendary Basque historical prose of the nineteenth century. As Jon Juaristi states, it is a return to the glorious past to restart it from the beginning (164). This nostalgia and romantic sentimentality became key in the reconstruction of Basque identity and in the creation of the imagined Basque community.

Minoritized works and authors also found a place in the magazine. Catalan, Breton, or Occitan literature was given a space in *Euzko-Gogoa*'s pages. Works of authors such as Miguel Costa i Llobera (1950), considered one of the leading representatives of Catalan poetry of all time, were translated. Per Denez (1950), a Breton author, and Bernart Manciet (1957), an Occitan author, among others, had works that were translated. It is interesting to see a peripheral language such as Basque translating other peripheral languages too, perhaps showing that there isn't a hierarchy among languages but rather that there should be equality and a voice for all.

Translations of works that showed social injustice were also published in *Euzko-Gogoa*. Despite not having a large percentage of articles related to social issues, the magazine did give a voice to various social classes. Basque working and agrarian classes as well as Guatemalan peasants also had their opinions published in the magazine. Although less prominent in the magazine, these translations showed the criticism of oppression, poverty, and power. For example, Martin Oiarzabal translated Henryk Sienkiewicz's *Ianko ereslari* (Janko the Musician, 1957). This story is based on the social injustice suffered by Ianko, a ten-year-old laborer, who is physically punished for touching the rebec, a medieval musical instrument, of a nobleman.

Most of the translations were literary works: poetry, narrative, and drama. However, some translations had a political tone, including *Sinisten dut askatasunean* (I Believed in Freedom), written by Zaitegi in 1956. It was an adaptation of the foundations of the U.S. Constitution. He highlighted the community effort of a country to work together toward a common goal. Jesuit Gotzon Garate adapted Anton Hilckman's *Europako erri zaarrena* (The Oldest Country in Europe) in 1959. The text discusses Basque history, language, culture, and traditions. The final paragraph stands out, particularly where Hilckman argues that the Basque Country was always free, a country never subjugated to the Spanish or French states: "This country, in all its history never was dominated. Everyone was free" (38). There is no doubt that the magazine had political concerns, even though literary themes defined the primary trajectory of the magazine. The magazine's political engagement will be analyzed later in more detail.

In the magazine, the reader can find the works of three women authors who were translated: Swedish Selma Lagerlöf, Scottish-Irish sister Nivedita, and Chilean Gabriela Mistral. It is important to analyze the background of these women because of the connection between nationalism and women, showing a stereotypical ideal woman. Josu Insausti translated Lagerlöf's *Gau donea* (Holy Night, 1954). The author recounts the great sadness that she experienced when she was five years old when her grandmother died, which made her remember a story that the old woman used to tell her about Holy Night. Although it is a moving story about compassion, the figure of the grandmother is shown as a transmitter of moral values, and a symbol of tradition and love. Lagerlöf was the first female writer to win the Nobel Prize in Literature in 1909. She was a leader in the women's suffrage movement and actively supported the resistance against the Nazis.

Nemesio Etxaniz translated Mistral's *Maitaxun ixilla* (Silent Love, 1956). Mistral was the first and still only Latin American woman who has received the Nobel Prize in Literature. Finally, Andima Ibiñagabeitia translated Nivedita's *Maitasun eta erio kantua* (An Indian Study of Love and Death, 1957). Ibiñagabeitia included an introduction explaining who Nivedita was as he lauded her:

> Nivedita was a Buddhist who lived in India during one of the hardest periods of the country. During colonial times, Sister Nivedita acted honestly in favor of the freedom of the country, with the strength and relentless weapon given by her desire of life. (56)

It's somewhat peculiar for the magazine to include, since it was much more connected to the Christian religion. This work analyzes the Buddhist mystic, whose beliefs neither coincide with nor contradict Christian dogma. However, the aim of the work is to delight readers as it could be good for their soul. As Ibiñagabeitia explained in the introduction to the translation: "It could do so much good to our soul" (56).

In these translated works, the characters share similar characteristics: a woman with a political and cultural ideology who advocates for the defense of cultural identity and for a change in the society. *Euzko-Gogoa* was a platform to demonstrate how capable women were and that they could be part of the magazine's canon. In the imagined community built in the magazine, they translated strong female figures. The role of women in the magazine will be further analyzed.

However, some Basque intellectuals harshly judged the translations made in the magazine because of their complexity of syntax and vocabulary. That created a confrontation between two groups of writers: those who saw in translation a pathway toward the normalization of the Basque language and others a lack of imagination. Koldo Mitxelena, the most influential intellectual and linguist of the Basque panorama from the 1960s to the 1980s and the person who led the process of unification of the Basque language, in the article "Asaba zaarren baratza" (The Old Patriots' Garden, 1960) published in *Egan,* criticized the excessive number of translations made into Basque:

> We have had so many translations since Basque literature began ... Although I don't think that they are very valuable. In cultured languages translations are very common. However, it's not translations that bring prestige to a language, but the original works. In the flourishing of literature the translations come along, as the tail comes after the body. The tail is not the body though; neither is the most important body part; in fact it is just an annex, shorter or longer, of the main body. We will impress foreigners when one of our works is translated to their language and not when we translate ten works from their language into Basque. (129)

Nevertheless, this strategy promoted in *Euzko-Gogoa* that Mitxelena criticized has been proven not to have had a negative impact on Basque literature, but rather quite the opposite. In fact, time has shown the inevitability of the importance of translations into Basque. Miren Ibarluzea, in her thesis *Itzulpengintzaren errepresentazioa euskal literatura garaikidean: eremuaren autonomizazioa, literatur historiografiak eta itzultzaileak fikzioan* (The Representation of Translation in the Contemporary Basque Literature: The Autonomy of Fields, Literary Historiographies and Fiction Translators), argues that the autonomization in the translation and the professionalization of translators have meant the restructuring of Basque literary translation, promoting a positive image of translators and their texts (124–125). Indeed, as her thesis shows, translations since the mid-twentieth century, when Basque literature began its process of autonomization, have had the goal of increasing the status of Basque literature. Translations, therefore, enrich Basque language, literature, and culture with other cultural and literary contributions. The following table lists the translations published in *Euzko-Gogoa* during its years in Guatemala, between 1950 and 1955:

Writer	Translation	Author	Genre	Year
Zaitegi, Jokin	Irukoitza (Terzett)	Joseph von Eichendorff	Poetry	1950
	Fomentor'ko lerrondoa (The Pine of Formentor)	Costa Llobera	Poetry	1950
	Epail eguna (Judgment Day)	Detlev von Liliencron	Poetry	1951
	Neska zapuztua (The Forsaken Maiden)	Eduard Mörike	Poetry	1951
	Nere atsekabe aundi (Out of My Great Unrest)	Heinrich Heine	Poetry	1951
	Goiz-eresia (Morning Song)	Ludwig Uhland	Poetry	1951
	Arroteztxeko alaba (The Landlady's Daughter)	Ludwig Uhland	Poetry	1951
	Bi gogoen eresia (The Song of Two Souls)	Richard Dehmel	Poetry	1951
	Begia (The Eye)	Sully-Prudhomme	Poetry	1952
	Mari Beltxa (Mary, the Black)	Pío Baroja	Tale	1952
	Angelus	Pío Baroja	Tale	1952
Mirande, Jon	Bi beleak (The Two Crows)	Unknown author, 17th century Ballad	Poetry	1950
	Ba-nin adiskide bat (I Had a Comrade)	Ludwig Uhland	Poetry	1950
	Lotazillak amabi (December Twelfth)	Per Denez	Poetry	1950
	Bela (The Raven)	Edgar Allan Poe	Poetry	1950
	Breiziera (Breton)	Per Denez	Article	1951

Writer	Translation	Author	Genre	Year
	Goiztar txoriek kanta bezate (The Morning Birds Will Sing)	Leon Jasson	Poetry	1951
	Ixiltze (Siope/Silence: A Fable)	Edgar Allan Poe	Tale	1951
	La Belle Dame sans merci	John Keats	Poetry	1952
	Amontillado Upela (The Cask of Amontillado)	Edgar Allan Poe	Tale	1952
	Lekhoreko biziarena (The Ballad of External Life)	Hugo von Hofmannsthal	Poetry	1954
	Legearen aitzinean (Before the Law)	Franz Kafka	Tale	1954
	Eros arrosen artean (Eros among Roses)	Pseudo Theocritus	Poetry	1954
Zaitegi-Ibiñagabeitia	Abere-indarra (Brute Force)	Jacinto Benavente	Drama	1950
Zatarain, Anbrozio	Balekiye (And If They Knew it…)	Heinrich Heine	Poetry	1950
Larrañaga, Eladio	Neguko ipuina (Winter's Tale)	William Shakespeare	Play	1950
	Lear Erregea (King Lear)	William Shakespeare	Play	1951
Labaien, Antonio M.	Linkeus dorrezaia (Faust –2nd part, 5th verse)	Johann Wolfgang von Goethe	Poetry	1951
Ametzaga, Bingen	Plini gaztearen idazkiak (The Letters of the Younger Pliny)	Pliny	Essay	1951
	Adiskidetasuna (De Amicitia)	Cicero	Essay	1952
	LXVI.garren amalaukoa (LXVI. Sonnet)	William Shakespeare	Poetry	1954

The Imagined Community Created in Euzko-Gogoa

Writer	Translation	Author	Genre	Year
	Reading baitegiko leloa (The Ballad of Reading Goal)	Oscar Wilde	Poetry	1954
Mokoroa, Justo M.	Erraondoko azken dan-bolinteroa (The Last Drummer of Erraondo)	Arturo Campión	Short Story	1952-1955
Insausti, Jesus	Zaldi zuriaren edestia (The Summer of the Beautiful White Horse)	William Saroyan	Short Story	1952
	Hanford'erako ibillaldia (The Journey to Hanford)	William Saroyan	Short Story	1952
	Gau donea (Holy Night)	Selma Lagerlöf	Short Story	1954
	Ibillaldietarako oarrak (Old Country Advice to the American Traveler)	William Saroyan	Short Story	1954
	Antzinako maitasun edesti bat (An Old Love Story)	William Saroyan	Short Story	1955
	Neskazarra (The Woman Who Was Loved)	James Stern	Short Story	1955
Sorrarain, Antonio	Itzaltzuko koblaria (The Bard of Itzaltzu)	Arturo Campión	Short Story	1954
Andima Ibiñagabeitia	Erleak eta eriotza (Bees and Death)	Garate Arriola	Article	1954
	Bergil'en Unai-Kantak (Bucolics)	Virgil	Poetry	1954
	Euskal mitologiaren ikaspiderako I–II (Lessons from Basque Mythology I–II)	Jose Miguel Barandiaran	Article	1954
	Euskal mitologiaren ikaspiderako III–IV (Lessons from Basque Mythology III–IV)	Jose Miguel Barandiaran	Article	1955
	Bergil'en Unai-Kantak (Bucolics)	Virgil	Poetry	1955

Writer	Translation	Author	Genre	Year
	Bergil'en Unai-Kantak (Bucolics)	Virgil	Poetry	1955
Aresti, Gabriel	CIX.garren Sonetoa (CIX. Sonnet)	William Shakespeare	Poetry	1954
	Gauontzak (The Owls)	Charles Baudelaire	Poetry	1954
	Udazken-kantuak (Autumn Song)	Paul Verlaine	Poetry	1954
	Ezer ez (Nothing)	Juan Ramón Jiménez	Poetry	1955
	Ilhargiari (To the Moon)	Johann Wolfgang von Goethe	Poetry	1955
Etxaide, Jon	Euskal-Elertia prantziskotarren kantauri barruan (Basque Literature in Franciscan Songs)	Luis Villasante	Article	1954
Irigoien, Alfonso	Gaitzetsia (The Rejected)	Jacinto Benavente	Play	1954
Iturrioz, Antonio	Alzateko Jauna (The Legend of Juan de Alzate)	Pío Baroja	Short Story	1955

Table 5: Translations published in Euzko-Gogoa 1950–1955.

The following table lists the translations published during Euzko-Gogoa's years in Biarritz, between 1955 and 1960.

Writer	Translation	Author	Genre	Year
Arrutza, Mikel	Efeso'ko Anderedeuna (The Widow of Ephesus)	Petronius	Short Story	1956
Mirande, Jon	Bi fraideak (The Two Monks)	Seamus O'Neill	Short Story	1956
	Zaldiz Zeruan (Ghost Riders in the Sky)	Stan Jones	Poetry	1957
	Burua (The Head)	Bernat Manciet	Short Story	1957

Writer	Translation	Author	Genre	Year
Etxaniz, Nemesio	Maitasun ixilla (Silent Love)	Gabriela Mistral	Poetry	1956
	Tellagorri (Zalacaín the Adventurer)	Pío Baroja	Short Story	1957
Onaindia, Santi	Enea'rena (Aeneid)	Virgil	Epic Story	1956
	Enea'rena (Aeneid)	Virgil	Epic Story	1957
Larrañaga, Guillermo	Mila ta bat gauetako ipuinak (One Thousand and One Nights)	N/A	Short Story	1956
	Mila ta bat gauetako ipuinak (One Thousand and One Nights)	N/A	Short Story	1957
	Mila ta bat gauetako ipuinak (One Thousand and One Nights)	N/A	Short Story	1958
	Izkuntza eta abenda (Language and Race)	Arturo Campión	Article	1959
Zinkunegi, Joseba	Kepa deunaren oilaskoa (Saint Peter's Chicken)	Henri Pourrat	Short Story	1956
	Kozko-muñoa (The Hill)	Jean Manduit	Short Story	1958
Zaitegi, Jokin	Sinisten dut askatasunean (I Believed in Freedom)	N/A	Article	1956
	Aiatz (Ajax)	Sophocles	Play	1957
	Piloktete (Philoctetes)	Sophocles	Play	1957
	Tarakin'go emaztekiak (Women of Trachis)	Sophocles	Play	1957
	Umezurtz (The Orphan)	Giovanni Pascoli	Poetry	1959
Jauregi, A.	Arrigorria'ko guda (The War of Arrigorriaga)	Sabino Arana	Legend	1956
Oiartzabal, Martin	Ianko ereslaria (Yanko the Musician)	Henryk Sienkiewicz	Short Story	1957

Writer	Translation	Author	Genre	Year
	Aosta'ko legenarduna (The Leper of Aosta)	Joseph Maistre	Play	1959
Ibiñagabeitia, Andima	Maitasun eta erio kantua (An Indian Study of Love and Death)	Sister Nivedita	Tale-Poetry	1957
Etxeberria, Frantzisko	Dabid'en eresiak XVII-garren (The Psalm of David)	Joseph Gelineau	Poetry	1957
	Dabid'en eresiak XLVII-garren (The Psalm of David)	Joseph Gelineau	Poetry	1957
Larrakoetxea, Bedita	Macbeth	William Shakespeare	Play	1957
	Lear Errege (King Lear)	William Shakespeare	Play	1958
	Ekatxa (The Tempest)	William Shakespeare	Play	1959
Erkiaga, Eusebio	Bei itsua (The Blind Cow)	Joan Maragall	Poetry	1958
Garate, Gotzon	Europako erri zaarrena (The Oldest Country in Europe)	Hilckmann	Article	1959
Juaristi, Migel	Adiskide zintzoa (The Devoted Friend)	Oscar Wilde	Short Story	1959
Mujika, Luis Mari	Pinotxo'ren biurriker-iak (The Adventures of Pinocchio)	Carlo Collodi	Short Story	1959
Ametzaga, Bingen	Prometeu burdinetan (Prometheus Bound)	Aeschylus	Play	1959
San Martin, Juan	Zeuk nai duzuna (Whatever You Want)	Juan Ramón Jiménez	Poetry	1959

Table 6: Translations published in Euzko-Gogoa 1956–1960.

Zaitegi and his fellow writers and contributors made certain that the use and development of the Basque language was their main priority. For them, the Basque language was the main pillar of the Basque nation and for the country to further develop and progress the Basque language would also need to adapt and grow. The Basque Country and its language were intrinsically connected. With the publication of *Euzko-Gogoa*, the Basque language was shown to be capable of sophisticated conversation and literature, and translations were an integral part of demonstrating its wealth. One can also see the subliminal messaging and mindset, the political orientation of the writers based upon the works translated. *Euzko-Gogoa* was a voice and a lobbyist for the need to standardize the Basque language to progress and adapt to a changing world. Zaitegi felt that all levels of society should promote and use the Basque language, especially the intellectual and high classes to give status and rank to the language. However, their support for enhanced Gipuzkoan and the translations made in the magazine were at the antipodes of reality and far from the literary and linguistic needs of the Basque readers in the Basque Country.

Furthermore, it should be noted that the canonic Basque writers of the Second Republic such as Lauxeta and Lizardi printed bilingual editions of their works. Although they were Basque nationalists, they were aware of the pragmatism of the Spanish language. On the other hand, *Euzko-Gogoa*'s "purist" linguistic approach, writing and publishing only in Basque, alienated many potential readers, not only readers who didn't know Basque but also others who could speak and read it. Zaitegi and Ibiñagabeitia were aware of this reality. Ibiñagabeitia in 1956 sent a letter to Zaitegi upset about the fact that Basque readers didn't want to read in Basque: "Basque writers have to face a reality that no other writers have to. We have to write to people who don't know and don't want to read in Basque."[43]

These strategies promoted in the magazine moved further away from the youngest generation of writers and readers. *Euzko-Gogoa* was in many ways anchored in the historic, nostalgic, and idealized Basque world, breathing from the memory of the prewar period. As Aldekoa refers to this issue, "In the sixties it (*Euzko-Gogoa*'s mindset) became a problem."[44] The new Basque reality and literature had to and wanted to break from the past and approach literature with new sensibilities.

Religion

Throughout *Euzko-Gogoa*'s existence, various texts discuss and refer to religion. Zaitegi was a Jesuit priest, along with Orixe and Ibiñagabeitia. Besides the founders, 54 percent of the authors and promoters of the magazine were priests. Also, many of the subscribers and readers were priests or religious figures. As the imagined community created by these authors, religion or religious values were an important part in creating a collective self-consciousness and identity.

THE BASQUE COUNTRY AS GOD'S BELOVED COUNTRY

One of the main arguments in the magazine was that the Basque Country was God's beloved country. In this regard, the magazine created an intrinsic relationship between Christianity and Basqueness. Andoni Arozena for instance, argued that because of the unique connection between Basques and God, the Basque Country was still relevant:[45]

> We can't lose hope! The Basques, thanks to God, have a strong will. If it wasn't that way, our identity would have been lost a long time ago. God took pity on us; because of that it seems he wants to give us relief in our path.

The magazine promoted the idea that being an honest Basque was to be Christian and *euskaltzale* (admirer of the Basque language and culture). In other words, good Basques should love God and the Basque Country: "If the Basque language kept us distinguished from the rest, and the clean and honest blood of the first Basque is still flowing in our veins, there isn't anyone as devoted as Basques."[46]

Because of this belief in an intrinsic relationship between God and Basques, the Basque language acquired a celestial value in the magazine, where the language and the idea of the eternal nature of God were united. The fate of the language was therefore connected to God's will. Gotzon Urrutia stated: "The Basque language will not die; what hasn't yet died will never die; God has given this immortal condition, as God has protected it until now and will forever."[47] The magazine portrayed God as having a special relationship with the Basque language and nation, giving them a supreme quality.

The idea of Basques being God's chosen ones was rooted in Basque society for centuries. For example, in the sixteenth century, authors such as Esteban de Garibay argued that Tubal, Noah's grandson, was the patriarch of the Basques. He settled in the Iberian Peninsula, and consequently his language, Basque, was the first spoken language in the peninsula. Joxe Azurmendi (1992, 19) collected the statements of Claudio Sánchez Albornoz, who was minister of state during the Spanish Second Republic and president of the Spanish government in exile from 1962 to 1970. Even the Spanish were aware of this belief among the Basques that they were connected to God. He said that the Basques were "crude people, simpletons, who believe that they are the children of God and heirs of His glory and yet they are no more than Spaniards who weren't Romanized."[48]

THE CHURCH

During the War of 1936, many of the priests who contributed to the magazine saw the human cruelty carried out in the name of God. The hypocrisy of the Spanish Catholic Church and its support of Spanish dictator Francisco Franco led many Basque religious members to lose their faith in the church itself. A strong statement made in the magazine was that the so-called "Holy War," the "War of Liberation," or the "Crusade" waged in the name of God by the Francoist troops was a lie. *Euzko-Gogoa* was critical of the war and especially of the church and the priests who supported it. The magazine saw in the ecclesiastical institution and in its elements an instrument of destruction and disintegration of Basque language and culture. Both the church and most of the Spanish priests were threatening the peace, stability, and security of the Basque nation. The magazine criticized the double-edged function of religion.

Orixe, through his essay *Quiton arrebarekin* (In Quito with my Sister, 1950–1954), wrote about the War of 1936. He analyzed the war in sections divided according to the events during and after the conflict. Sectioned as *Infernua* (Hell), *Matxinada* (Uprising), *Naparroa lotsagarriena* (Navarre, the Most Disgraceful), *Lotsagarrien lotsagarriena* (The Most Disgraceful of the Disgraceful), *Castiella* (Castile), *Illentzat ere gorrotoa* (Hatred even to those that are already death) and *Gurutze Guda* (Crusade). Through these sections, Orixe gave a personal view of the war, the experiences he lived through, and the things he saw. Orixe didn't want the events of the war to pass into oblivion or to be misinterpreted. He knew the fate of those who didn't have a chance to escape. He gave voice to the agonizing pain of witnessing the killing of his family, friends, and culture in the name of God: "They stole His name and carried the flag of Satan" (49). Orixe argues that since Basques fought on the losing side, there is hatred toward Basques as a result. Unfortunately, this hatred also appears after the war and, according to Orixe, will continue to be felt. Orixe feels utter disgust and a sense of disbelief that this is a reality and that religion, and the name of God, are used to punish a society.

The Spanish Church appears as one of the main antagonists to the Basque language. The hatred of the church toward the Basque language resonates on the pages of *Euzko-Gogoa*: "The Church is the enemy and destroyer of the Basque language: the priests are trying to take away the Basque language from ecclesiastical life."[49] In "Irakurlearen Txokoa," the magazine said that it would not remain silent in the face of the persecution against the Basque language carried out by the clergy:[50]

> To say nothing of the injustices against our language is counter-productive: because if you remain silent you allow it; and we don't want people to think that we agree with this maliciousness. We don't have enough circulation; this is true, too. But we don't have any other way to make our voices heard, and we always do so in Basque. They don't want to listen to us? The deaf and despicable are everywhere, especially in our country. Nevertheless, this is not going to stop our work.

Franco and the Spanish Church won the war together, and they managed the "peace" with the repressive forces of the state. The church recovered the leading role in the educational system following the War of 1936, where the principles of Catholic dogma were instructed. The new education imposed by Franco's regime was based on forming loyal and Christian students of the "new" Spain. In this regard, the Catholic Church held great power over the field of education. Jaime Kerexeta, in his article "Euzkeraren alde" (In Favour of the Basque Language, 1955), strongly criticized the role of clerics, priests, and nuns in the Southern Basque Country undermining the Basque language. He condemned their hatred against the language: "Where does such hatred of the Basque language come from by priests and nuns?" (17). He also denounced their methods of punishment to eradicate the use of Basque in schools: "Lekaide lekaime irakasleak: badakigu Eskoriatza ta Elorrio'ko Marianista-ikastetxetan, adibidez, mutikoak euzkeraz egitearren ainbat bidar jolas-tokietan ormari begira belauniko egon dirana" [(1–2), 17] [Priests and nuns who teach: we know that in the towns of Eskoriatza and Elorrio at the religious school, the children who speak in Basque are punished by having to kneel while facing the wall]. The Spanish Church blessed Franco's uprising, and after Franco's victory the Church received the support of the government in the "re-catholicization" of the country after its secularization during the Second Republic. Actually, Ander Gurruchaga states: "The Church becomes the principal ally of Franco in his politics of institutionalization and justification of his new social order" (143).[51] According to Francoist views, it was the War of 1936 that sustained the Christian and Spanish spirit against the "other spirit," non-Spanish and non-Christian.

These actions contributed to the growing frustrations of the Basque population toward the Church, and therefore led to continued animosity in the writings of *Euzko-Gogoa*. Despite having translations and writings with religious tone and subject matter, rarely does one read of praise for the Spanish Catholic Church.

MYTHOLOGY AND PAGANISM

The magazine was also a place for ideas on paganism, mythology, and heterodoxy. Mythology has always had a great impact in Basque culture, even when Christianity was introduced. The Christian religion and paganism actually coexisted for centuries in the Basque Country. Such deep-rooted stories and rituals are a large part of Basque culture, and *Euzko-Gogoa* helped share these supernatural and pagan stories. Jon Mirande wrote some poems and stories on the topic, including *Akelarre* (Coven, 1950), where he talked about the pagan rituals carried out by witches during a witches sabbath. He also wrote about the first Basque God, Urtzi, in the poem *Ortzi'ren ttunttuna* (Ortzi's Drum, 1952). Before Christianity, the Basque people looked to the sky for their God. The poem *Cantemus Domino* (Let Us Sing unto the Lord, 1950), written by Imanol

Arriandiaga, was also about Urtzi. Jon Etxaide, in the story *Arangio'ko basalorea* (The Wild Flower of Arangi, 1952), talked about the relationship between a man and a *lamia*, a Basque water nymph. The Basques worshipped what they had in front of them: the earth, the sky, the sun, the moon, and nature in general. The magazine considered Basque mythology an important cornerstone of Basque identity, a fundamental element for nation building. In fact, the works of José Miguel Barandiaran about Basque mythology were translated into the Basque language too. Despite the Christianization experienced by the Basque people, mythology carries an important weight in the stories or elements that build the religious, mythical identity of a community.

In addition, other religions such as Buddhism were described in the magazine with Mirande's *Beiak* (Cows, 1951) and Sister Nivedita's *Maitasun eta erio kantua* [The Song of Love and Death]. Their inclusion raises several questions: Was it to showcase other realities and inform the reader of cultures new to them? Was it an attempt to show the globalization process and that there is life beyond Catholicism and the Basque Country and to give its readers an enjoyable text?

Before the War of 1936, many Basques had a strong faith and close ties to the Catholic Church. Seeing the atrocities of war in the name of God carried out by Franco's troops with the support of the Church, Basques felt deceived. Olaziregi and Otaegi state that many of the postwar writers lived divided by incompatible loyalties to the humiliated homeland and the victorious ecclesiastical hierarchy to which they owed obedience (2011, 47). Like Jesus Christ betrayed by Judas, Basques felt they had been betrayed and that their culture was being punished and condemned. However, they had a strong faith in God despite the loss of trust in the church. With these preconceived notions of being God's chosen ones, they carried their cross and suffered, knowing that in the end they would prevail. Many sought a life in exile, like the exodus of Moses with the belief that they would be protected and that their opportunity to return would arise in the future. They found in God the comfort and strength to overcome their agony. With references to the pre-Christian and pagan culture of the Basque world, mythology, and other religions, they felt a connection with their tradition, roots, and broader spirituality.

Women

In previous studies of *Euzko-Gogoa*, the impact of the women involved with the magazine has been overlooked. These individuals have been hidden figures for too long. The cultural work of Basque women during Franco's regime, and more specifically during the 1950s, deserves to be analyzed. This section will focus on the various women who collaborated in the magazine and what was written in the magazine in reference to women and motherhood as well as determine how the image of the woman was constructed in the pages of the magazine.

Although there were Basque women writers long before, it was not until the beginning of the twentieth century that women began to have a place in the Basque literary arena. It was in the early 1900s that many institutional and cultural platforms were developed, for example the creation of EAB—Emakume Abertzale Batza (Association of Nationalist Women 1922–23). The EAB brought with it many changes for Basque women by redefining their identity and their place. These women went from village to village spreading the EAJ-PNV ideology and, more specifically, a woman's role inside the party. Through these interventions, women gained a public voice for the nationalist ideal, gradually entering an environment previously monopolized by men. As Mercedes Ugalde states, their work was to create propaganda campaigns in favor of the EAJ-PNV and to organize events related to cultural education, social assistance, and charity.[52] Education and cultural values were the main areas of concern for women of EAB.

During these changing times when women were gaining a voice in politics, they were also becoming more active in the literary community. For the Basques, literature and politics during this period were often related. The Basque literature of the twentieth century was described by Amaia Alvarez (2005, 50) as "Lehen loraldia" (The first awakening): "It was the time of Basque nationalism, the defense of religion/faith and the Basque language. With regard to women, a patriotic motherly image was promoted."[53] Before the War of 1936, there were many cultural activities in the Basque Country promoted by Euskaltzaleak (an association created in 1930 with the aim of cultivating and promoting the Basque language and culture from folklore) in which many women participated. Also, many magazines published before the war, such as *Euskalerriaren Alde* (In Favor of the Basque Country), *Euzkerea* (The Basque Language), *Bizkaitarra* (The Biscayan), *Amayur,* and *Aberri Eguna* (The Day of the Motherland) included contributions from various female writers. Some of the women writers of those years were Petra Belaustegi, Maria Artiñao, Katalina Elizegi, Tene Mujika, Karmele Errazti, Errose Bustintza, Sorne Unzueta, Julene Azpeitia, and Elbira Zipitria. Although fewer than those published by male authors, many books were published by women between 1900 and 1934, including Katalina Elizegi's *Garbiñe* (Purification, 1916), *Loreti* (Garden, 1918), and Julene Azpeitia's *Osasuna, merketza ta yanaritzaz* (Health, Business and Food, 1922).

Mikel Atxaga argues that women authors who were able to write in Basque did so because they had an academic background (1997, 6). The women writers came from similar, almost identical backgrounds; almost all of them were teachers and were married to a writer, politician, academic, or businessman. As Virginia Woolf states in her classic essay: "A woman must have money and a room of her own if she is to write fiction" (1989, 4). Amaia Alvarez enumerates the features of these women: "The profile of the Basque women writers is the following: teachers, activists, or relatives of a writer or poet."[54] Above all, they used to be around the church, the *batzoki* (Basque Nationalist Party community center), and the school. However, because of the War of 1936, many of these women were forced to go into exile because of their involvement with the EAJ-PNV. It was from exile that some of them continued working in support of the Basque language. In this regard, *Euzko-Gogoa* gave these women a platform to maintain the Basque language while also opening the door for their entrance into the literary canon.

THE ARCHETYPAL NATIONALIST WOMAN

Euzko-Gogoa promoted an ideal Basque nationalist woman. Through its publication, it advocated for a pure, almost virginal woman. She would be patriotic, Christian, and fulfill the task of preserving, spreading, and nurturing the Basque language and love for the motherland to her children, because those children were the future of the nation and the future torchbearers of the Basque language. In the pages of *Euzko-Gogoa,* as well as in the Basque political arena, it was a fundamental precept that women take on greater responsibility for teaching their children the Basque language. As Thiong'o states, language is the symbol of a person's soul and an inseparable tool of any human community.[55] The transmission of the mother tongue is crucial to keeping national identity alive.

Sorne Unzueta, Karmele Errazti, Julene Azpeitia, Miren Ibargutxi, and Engratzi Iñurrieta were the five women who wrote for the magazine. In addition to the importance of the image of motherhood conveyed in *Euzko-Gogoa*, this section will also focus on the life and works of Unzueta, Errazti, and Azpeitia; there is limited information on Ibargutxi and Iñurrieta. It appears that the last two authors did not continue writing cultural or literary works following their contributions to the magazine.

Unzueta, her pen name "Utarsus," was a political activist during the Basque nationalist movement of the early twentieth century. She was a teacher, a member of EAB, a writer, a mother, and more. She shared the EAJ-PNV's ideology in meetings throughout the Basque Country and was a well-known demagogue in the party. According to Igone Etxebarria: "Her party conferences were vehement" (2000, 8).[56] However, when the uprising began in 1936, she was forced into exile and moved to France. Once there, she was an active member of the resistance during the Second World War. She was the only woman of the resistance group, in which her husband also participated. Etxebarria explains Sorne's very dangerous task: "Sorne's job was to carry messages from the free zone to the area occupied by the Nazis."[57] After more than a decade in exile, in 1953, she returned to the Southern Basque Country with her family.

Unzueta published two works in the magazine, the first of which was *Itxartu, euzko-alabea* (Wake up Basque Daughter, 1950), a poem with a nationalistic and propagandistic discourse. The scholar Maite Nuñez-Betelu calls it a "a pamphlet poem" (2001, 143). The poem was a call to action for increased participation of women in the national struggle: "¿Eta ondiño lo-zagoz, / Ene aizta kutuna? / ¿Etzaitu ondiño itxartu / Lanaren zarateak? / ¡Itxartu, euzko-alaba, / Jagi, emakumia!" [Are you still sleeping / my beloved sister? / The noise of the work / didn't wake you up? / Wake up Basque-daughter / Wake up, Women!] (my trans.; 14–16). This call to resistance against the Spanish regime is similar to what Frantz Fanon promotes for colonized cultures. For Fanon, literature should be used as a tool to awaken the mentality of the subjugated communities.[58]

In the poem, Unzueta also mentions the founding father of the EAJ-PNV, Sabino Arana: "Sabin, gure neba onak, / Lenengua entzun eban" (14–16) [Sabino, our good Brother / he was the first one to hear the call]. Unzueta promoted a proactive relationship between women and nation, while always completing her assigned role. Unzueta recognized and accepted the minor role of women in politics. Maite Nuñez-Betelu explains:

> Regarding the situation of women, *Utarsus* advocates for the equality of women and men as regards their participation in the patriotic struggle. Men and women must participate equally in the fight, but each one fulfilling their corresponding role as it is marked by their gender. (149)

Unzueta's second work published in the magazine was the patriotic poem, *Artxanda*, 1952. Unzueta examined the relationship between a mother and her son. As Etxebarria explains, maternity is one of the pillars of Unzueta's work: "In Unzueta's works, the relationship between mother and children, a mother's feelings, and what a mother should teach her children are themes that appear frequently" (16). The poem showed the reality that many mothers faced during the War of 1936: the sorrow of letting their sons fight for the motherland, the loss of the war, the fate of their sons at the hands of the enemy, the emptiness, and lost identity. The title of the poem is also significant. Artxanda is a mountain of Bilbao, and it was the place where the *gudaris* (Basque army soldiers) made a "suicidal" counterattack against the Francoist troops before the inevitable fall of Bilbao. This battle allowed the general population to escape Franco's troops and leave the city.

The defeat of the city and the fate of the soldiers taken in Artxanda was embraced in the poem through the conversation between mother and son: "The enemy had taken / our youth / poor things! / they are taking them to the slaughterhouse / they will soon be up against the wall / oh, my dear son / murdered by the weapon / they will fall . . ." [(3–4), 4].[59] The intrinsic relationship between mother, son, and motherland should be noted. Nerea Aresti (2014, 305) collects statements made by Polixene Trabudua, an active member of EAB, about the pain and emotional control of Basque mothers seeing their sons going to war: "When they saw the *gudaris* leave, they limited themselves to directing their humble gaze as Basque mothers and perhaps because they do not know how to kiss, hug, or cuddle, they put into that gaze all the treasure of their soul."[60] It shows how much they loved not only their homeland but their sons. Rather than attempting to be emotional, these mothers accepted the reality of the situation knowing they could see both their sons and country lost. The role of women in general and mothers in particular is always that of an assistant. There is no female agency; in fact, feminine characters are mainly secondary and mostly helpers to a male.

Errazti was the first president of EAB. She was also an active writer in the nationalist press, using the pseudonyms "Etxakin" and "Emakume batek" [which translate to "Unknown" and "A Woman," respectively]. She was married to Basque writer Keperin Xemein. She was exiled in Pau, France, during the War of 1936 and never came back to the Southern Basque Country. In *Euzko-Gogoa*, she wrote two works: an obituary about the death of Basque patriots "Juan yakuzan bixitz oroigarrijak" (They Left Us, 1951) and a letter titled "Euzko-Gogoa" (Basque-Will, 1950), where she highlighted the good work done by the magazine, especially in encouraging the use of the Basque language:[61]

> Zaitegi has shown that it is possible to write in Basque about the deepest topics. His beautiful magazine *Euzko-Gogoa* arrives in every corner of the world; it will have so many Basque readers and these readers will be reading in a good and correct Basque and not in a bad Basque.

Nuñez-Betelu states that Errazti tried through her writings to educate children to love God, the Basque nation, and the Basque language.[62] Errazti was very active in EAB and very pro-Sabino in her ideology. According to Sabino Arana's view, women should be the most important figures in the promotion of language and culture, hence the rationale for why Erratzi was so focused on the use of correctly written Basque.

In 1952, in the issue 3–4, Errazti's husband, Xemein, wrote an article explaining how a married couple (referring to himself and Errazti) writing in the magazine together:[63]

I know a couple who writes in Basque in the magazine. Both were writers before they got married. Since then they have published so many works. The wife began to write before the husband. And both of them write using the same typewriter. A word to the wise is sufficient.

His comments could be interpreted as very pro-women by showing the equality within the couple. He shows how there is no jealousy and that both can be capable of working together toward a common goal.

Azpeitia, who signed her work with her pen name "Arritokieta," [name of the hermitage in the town of Zumaia] was one of the main writers who defended Basque traditions, especially the importance of education in the Basque language. Azpeitia was a vocational teacher whose main priority was to create an educational model to use with Basque children for promoting the Basque language. Laura Mintegi collected the words of Azpeitia: "The country, the whole country that speaks in Basque, has to know both oral and written Basque if it's going to be living in Basque" (7). For Azpeitia the Basque language was strongly bound to the nation and, like her fellow contributors, felt the language was essential for a future nation. In *Euzko-Gogoa*, she wrote "Goizeko izarra" (The Morning Star, 1959), a Christmas-themed tale, where it is possible to appreciate her interests: children, the Basque language, and religion. In 1975, Azpeitia received a tribute from Euskaltzaindia (The Royal Academy of Basque Language); she was nominated as an honorary member of the academy.

Like Unzueta and Errazti, Azpeitia was an active member of EAB, and she also promoted the secondary position of women in EAJ-PNV. Nuñez-Betelu states: "Azpeitia defends the gendered separation of roles within the party and accepts the role reserved for women."[64] Because of her involvement with the EAB, she was forced into exile when the war began. When she returned to the Basque Country in 1947, she was banished from the Basque Country and sent to Burgos (Spain) by Franco's regime in 1949 as punishment.

The other two female writers in the magazine were Miren Arrate Ibargutxi, who used the pen name "Miren-A," and Engratzi Iñurrieta "Sagar-Erreka." [Apple-River]. Ibargutxi wrote three poems "Bakarrik," "Negarrez," "Zoriontsu" ("Alone," "Crying," "Happy," 1958); "Euskal-Erriko mendietan" ("In the Mountains of the Basque Country," 1959); and "Zaude lo, kutuna" ("Sleep, My Dear," 1959). Iñurrieta wrote a poem "Kartzelako'aren ongi-etorria" ("The Welcoming of the Prisoner," 1956). These poems talk about the Basque nation, the beauty of nature, emotions, and love. Nevertheless, the literary path of these women didn't continue beyond the magazine.

Unzueta, Errazti, and Azpeitia are clear examples of the literature and actions promoted by Basque women at the beginning of the twentieth century.

Their educational work was relevant in the transmission of the Basque language, Basque traditions, and motherhood. Arrieta argues (2015b, 5) that in this eagerness to preserve the Basque language, the women were able to move on to new social spheres. For the first time they were able to teach the Basque language and traditions to the community. They taught classes to the elderly in the Basque Nationalist Party's social centers in the neighborhood schools and in the first Basque schools. Their participation in patriotic and political activities was also important, but always in their assumed "secondary" role to complement the work done by men. Mercedes Ugalde states that women's activities were more focused on collaboration in defense of the Basque language, emotional-assistance support, and collaboration in propaganda for nationalist politics.[65] The role of these women was closely linked to motherhood, as well as to faith and patriotism. Etxebarria explains: "Women are happy and proud of being a woman, and they see their role as mothers of the family."[66] Therefore, during this time, women weren't necessarily focused on being writers because their priorities were family duties.

During the 1950s, there were still relatively few Basque women writers. The movement of women writers that began at the start of the twentieth century was suspended because of the War of 1936. Many of them went into exile, and only a few continued writing. In 1954, in the issue 3–4, in the section "Irakurlearen Txokoa" or Readers Corner, one of the readers wondered why women did not write in the magazine, and Andima Ibiñagabeitia answered:

> Why don't women write for the magazine? This is what I am asking myself. Why don't they write in the Basque language? Our doors are open if they want to write, however, only one came to us "Emakume bat" [A Woman] a good patriot and an honest woman. Before, there used to be very good Basque women writers: Julene Azpeitia, Tene, Zipitria, etc. Errose Mañari just passed away. Does anyone want to publish an anthology of her work? It would be a good and appropriate thing to do. This last question, as always, will disappear in the desert without an answer. Shame on us! But let's continue talking about women writers. Why they don't write in Basque. Maybe they are busy teaching Basque to their children and they don't have time to be writing. If that is true, they will be forgiven; there is nothing more beautiful. However, I am afraid that they are speaking in Spanish. Women, when are you going to put all your efforts into speaking Basque? If you wanted to, our language would improve and develop: the tender lips of women have a special capacity for language. (68–69)[67]

The ideal form of womanhood was shown to be the ideal Basque mother:

a woman who carried with her traditional values and the Basque language. Although their writing skills were welcomed, motherhood was esteemed to be their primary value. Motherhood was still considered the primordial characteristic of a woman. Margaret Bullen (2003, 197–201) analyzes the intrinsic relationship between Basque women and nationalism, focusing on the works of Teresa del Valle, Mercedes Ugalde, Begoña Aretxaga, and Joseba Zulaika. These works show that in the system of contemporary Basque nationalism in the EAJ-PNV as well as in ETA (Basque Country and Freedom) before its cessation of armed activity, the figure of women was based on the traditional role of the mother.

Ibiñagabeitia appeared critical of the use of the Spanish language, which increased in the Basque population because of the social changes that the Basque Country underwent with the rise in the number of Spanish immigrants who came during the industrialization period. In this regard, in the eyes of many Basque nationalists, the Spanish language and the city were considered to be a bad influence on Basque women who were substituting the Spanish language for the Basque language. For them, Basque women were the transmitters of the Basque language to their children, and therefore the survival of the language was in their hands. Nerea Aresti demonstrates how EAJ-PNV tried to encourage women to stay in their rural areas: "Given this threat, it seemed necessary to address the beautiful daughters of the mountain and invite them to leave the cities and return home, to the traditional life of the race."[68] They tried to create propaganda for a more romanticized view of the "purer" women of the rural Basque Country, where they spoke in Basque and avoided the "contamination" of Spanish influence. This is in total confluence with the costumbrist prose exemplified by Txomin Agirre at the beginning of the twentieth century.

Ibiñagabeitia's statements were not the only ones that denounced women's inclination toward the Spanish language. Antonio M. Labaien argued in his article "Euskeraren kinka gaiztoa" (The Crisis of the Basque Language, 1958) that some women considered the Basque language vulgar and to seem more sophisticated they preferred to use the Spanish language, even though they came from rural areas. Jaime Kerexeta, in his article, stated:[69]

> Women, with their natural frivolity have the tendency to speak in Spanish, especially those who are feisty (we have to admit that women are vain in general, mostly before they get married). But once they get married, husbands, you have to keep in mind that you are the head of the family, and you have to be firm with your decisions, that they have to teach and speak Basque to the children.

The prejudice of female inferiority with respect to men is noteworthy. His opinion is one in which a woman improves once she gets married, and that wives' and mothers' primary tasks should be based on the transmission, speaking, and teaching of the Basque language. Kerexeta was a Franciscan priest, and his Catholic traditionalism is made evident in his text. Despite the criticism of women's tendency to use the Spanish language, the magazine tried to promote and motivate women to participate. The truth was that there were good women writers who showed their ability before the War of 1936 began, and one of the main objectives of the magazine was to be a network and meeting place for Basque writers.

The transmission of the Basque language by women was central to the ideal female image portrayed in the magazine. Also, in the imagined community created in *Euzko-Gogoa*'s pages, the ideal Basque woman had to be patriotic, proactive in the fight for the country (within her limitations), honest, pure, and above all she had to speak Basque. Other examples that demonstrate this representative Basque woman can be viewed in the following texts.

In "Amerika-Erdi ta Karibe'ko VI'garren Olinpiar Yolasak" (The 6th Caribbean Olympic Games, 1950), the author details the events of three Basque sisters who participated in the Sixth Caribbean Olympic games and praises their abilities as athletes and their qualities as Basque patriots. The author explains that they should be the model for Basque people, as they are outstanding not just in their words, using the Basque language, but in their winning medals:[70]

> We welcomed in Guatemala the sisters Bibiñe, Ibone and Osane that came to play the Caribbean Olympic Games from Mexico. They came as part of the Mexican team with their parents. During the games, the name of our compatriots was everywhere. The three sisters stirred up Guatemala. Everyday the Basque surname Belaustegigoitia touched our hearts . . . They showed the great capacity of Basques to play sports. What was most surprising was the fact that they were speaking Basque everywhere and at any time: Basque children everywhere, you should take these three sisters as an example to follow: beautiful in their words and even more beautiful in their actions.

It is remarkable to observe how these three Basque sisters were acknowledged, not just as good athletes, but as good Basques by constantly using their mother language. For *Euzko-Gogoa*, they were an example for Basque youth all over the world.

An exemplary Basque woman, according to Zaitegi, can be found in Orixe's book *Euskaldunak* [The Basques]. Zaitegi actually wrote an article called "'Orixe' ren 'Euskaldunak'" (1950). In Orixe's poem, one of the most significant plots is the love story between Garazi and Mikel. Zaitegi's article references the relationship between the two; he acknowledges the image Orixe created of the ideal Basque female, "Garazi." Garazi, which would be translated as "Grace," is described as a beautiful Christian girl. She reminds us of Malen, the devoted grandaugther of Joanes, the main character of *Garoa* (Fern, 1912), the costumbrist novel written by Txomin Agirre: "Her eyes always absorbent / she took God in the morning / and His memory in the middle of her heart / she is meditating / A shadow—she doesn't know what it is— / she has in her face / if it appeared in the world / Grace, who is an Angel" (7–8), 11. According to Basque scholar Ana Toledo, Garazi (Grace) is a static character typical of how women were portrayed during this period. She explains that in costumbrist literature, the main characters represented have three common denominators: they are Basque, Christian, and honest. These characteristics are forged under the motto, "Euskaldun, Fededun" (Basque and Faithful).[71] Zaitegi states at the end of the article that the entire Basque Country is represented in the poem: shepherds, woodchoppers, sailors, farmers, men, and women of the Basque Country described in the routines of their everyday life (12). Again, a folkloric and romanticized idea of a rural Basque community is created where women are angelic, virginal, patriotic, and Basque.

Zaitegi also wrote about Madame de Staël, in the article "Staël anderea (1766–1817)" (Madame de Staël 1766–1817, 1951), Zaitegi praises de Staël's human and intellectual qualities. He described her work *De l'Allemagne* as the new gospel of aesthetics: "You have written the gospel of the new aesthetic" (13). He argued that she was a strong woman, more courageous than many men, who went into exile because her ideas were opposed by Napoleon. For Zaitegi, she was a pioneer in all that she proposed, an intellectual and a modern woman:

> She stirred things up, she opened new pathways that were necessary for the language, she arranged the Romantic movement pathway so everyone could see God's treatment. (13)

Another interesting feminine figure that appeared in the magazine was Judith. Gotzon Egaña praised what Judith did for her people and country: "Judith has a good foundation, has blood, has a fascinating femininity. Her heart appears in flames, full of religiosity, flowing with patriotism, pure, strong, decisive."[72] Egaña represents Judith as a heroine who acted for the common good of her people by murdering Holofernes, who, through her actions, saved Israel. She fought against the enemies of Israel, all while showing her moral strength and love for her homeland. In the article, the writer shows how she was a strong and courageous woman:

> When she heard that the enemies would destroy her country, Judith didn't cower. She stood up proudly and, with patriotism, she changed her widow clothes and she dressed up the brightest ones and with the help and light of God she went to the camp of her enemies. (82)

Egaña compares Judith to other biblical women such as Esther, Ruth, and Rebekah, the epitome of humble, polite, brave, and loyal women. On the other hand, he argues that she was nothing like Delilah or Jezebel, creating a binary system of what made a woman good or bad. However, the perception of Judith may be ambiguous, since she can be interpreted as a biblical heroine, but also as a predatory woman as vampire or femme fatale. Indeed, as Daniela Hermisillo states, the fact that Judith killed Holofernes by cutting off his head and not poisoning him shows violence and bloodshed. These characteristics related to the image of the vampire woman, originating in the sixteenth century and so represented in art and literature, particularly by French symbolism and romanticism. Fundamentally, the political and cultural emancipation of women, which was beginning to develop in a society still determined by the French Revolution and the leading role of men, began to be reflected in a fearful male vision that basically reduced woman to two variants: the virtuous and asexual wife or the perverse, seductive femme fatale. In *Euzko-Gogoa*, she is represented as the virtuous and asexual wife.

The Basque nationalist imagination created the archetype of Basque women, based on the Basque versus Spanish dichotomy. Nerea Aresti argues that the virile restraint and the emotional austerity imprinted on the Basque woman distinguished her from the gestural voluptuousness and the expressive excess of the Spanish woman.[73] Egaña's text is the allegory of Basque women, as strong, temperate, and contained women like Judith.

The magazine promoted a woman who, in the family and even the social environment, should work for the survival and endurance of the Basque language and, in addition to her maternal and educational function, should be ready to defend her homeland. Madame de Staël and Judith became the paradigms of heroines that reflected the complexity of the gender vision in the magazine: strong, "independent," intellectual, and vehement women, but also highlighting the imposed assumption of women's weakness and temptation.

MOTHER (VIRGIN MARY) AND MOTHERLAND

The images of the mother, Holy Mother, and the motherland became key in the allegorical representation of Basque women in the magazine. The Basque Country is represented as a female or mother for the Basques. In the work "Opariz" (Gift, 1950), in the first issue of *Euzko-Gogoa*, Zaitegi wrote how the magazine was dedicated to the beloved motherland by her devoted sons:[74]

> This magazine, beloved Basque Country, we offer to you, because you are in the deepest will of our dreams: we offer you our efforts and our honest intentions, willing promotion and freedom. We who want to be your devoted sons, beloved homeland, God knows we are more

dedicated to you than to any other on earth. If it is necessary, we are ready to offer the warm blood of our veins for you. Because we have not forgotten what Sabino Arana said: "We for Euzkadi and Euzkadi for God."

Written by Koldo Jauregi Jautarkol, the poem "Anai-arteko gudatean" (The War Between Brothers, 1952) shows the sorrow of the motherland, during the War of 1936, seeing her sons fighting amongst themselves: "Poor Mother . . . / When all your sons / who love you so much? / How long / will you live / suffering for your sons?"[75]

The figure of the motherland was used in different texts of the magazine, comparing love for nation and language, to love for the mother. The article written by Errexil, "Euzko-Gogoa'ri buruz" (About Euzko-Gogoa, 1950), was an example: "The language we love as much as our mother, we should preserve it, save it, and immortalize it.[76] This form of writing created the sensation of what Basques should feel for their country, a commitment to the one who gave birth to you, gave you language and quality of life. This obligation to one's country is like a relationship with one's mother, where the individual is grateful and must honor, protect, and nurture the relationship.

Together with the motherland, the purity of the Basque mother and her role in nation building was developed in the magazine. For *Euzko-Gogoa*, the mother is the carrier of the language, and the Basque nation was an extension of her. Ziriako Andonegi, in the poem *Euskera maitea* (Beloved Basque Language, 1957), stated that the Basque language was a pure and beautiful language, transmitted by mothers to children. Nemesio Etxaniz, in the poem *Ama!* (Mother! 1952), represented the Basque mother as the axis and the soul of the Basque family: "During the long and dark nights of winter / when blizzards prevail / I have my Mother in mind, / I have my Mother in my heart."[77] Nerea Aresti argues that the Basque mother was associated with the special mission, which was to make the future generation faithful servants of the patriotic ideal.[78] The Basque mother was in charge of the transmission of Basque identity (Basque language, love for the motherland, tradition) and instilling religious piety.

The image of the Virgin Mary had great symbolic power in the magazine as well. This image was very much connected to the Basque mother, as an allegorical celestial representation of the earthly mother. The magazine portrays the character of a prudent woman, contained, without weaknesses, pure, sexless, and strong. The images of *Ama Birjina* (Mary, Mother of Jesus), *Begoñako Ama* (the Virgin of Begoña), and *Dolorezko Ama* (the Mother of Sorrows) appeared with a powerful meaning in different texts of the magazine.

Joseba Zulaika states (2014, 126) that the entire Marian religion is complex, with its very erotic structure of motherly sublimation and filial sacrifice. The Basque mother appears in some of the magazine's articles as the symbolic figure of the Mother of Sorrows, representing the consolation and support for her Basque children who were on their own *via crucis* (way of the cross). One can see this representation in the poem written by Mitxelena, *Guruz bidea euskal-samiñaren* (The Way of the Cross: the Cry of Basque Sorrow, 1955): "The clamor of Basque sorrow: / Goodbye, worried Mother of Sorrows / by our compassion / the tired Country!"[79] The image of the Mother of Sorrows was pervasive and had an important meaning in the idealization of how Basque women should live, according to the magazine. Miren Llona argues (2000, 193) that "the female model that appears associated with this divine figure is a woman who participates and who gains her right to share suffering but also the glory of men who give their lives for their country."[80] *Euzko-Gogoa* created an image of a woman who would be willing to sacrifice for her children and therefore her country.

The Virgin of Begoña, lovingly called by the Basques *amatxu* (mommy), is often referenced in the various writings in *Euzko-Gogoa*. She is the patron saint of Bilbao and Bizkaia and "a seafaring Virgin." Balendin Aurre-Apraiz wrote a poem honoring *Begoñako Ama* called *Gaurik gogorrena* (The Hardest Night, 1952): "From the groin to my foot / with eight wounds, / . . . / I prayed to the Virgin Mother of Begoña."[81] Here he is seeking the help of the Virgin during times of pain, which appears to be based during war time. The writer G. E. A, through the following poem *Begoña'ko Ama neskutz bizkaitarren zaindarijari* (To the Virgin of Begoña protector of the Bizkaians, 1952), expressed his admiration for this Virgin: "Mother Virgin of Begoña / Pure Mother of God / beautiful flower of Heaven / star of the sea / since ancient times the Bizkaians / have chosen you as our Patron Saint."[82] She is the personification of Bizkaia and its savior mother.

The Virgin Mary, the most venerated woman, myth, and object of devotion, was admired throughout the magazine. Balendin Aurre-Apraiz wrote the poem *Sortzez garbiari* (To the Pure from Birth, 1951): "Mommy who is pure from birth / my beloved and soft Mommy / I bend my knee before you / begging for help."[83] Many other authors also dedicated verses to the Virgin Mary. She was the representation of the sacrifice undergone by a mother, allowing her son to die for the common good. This is very much connected to the statement made by Polixene Trabudua, in which the Basque mother, although torn with pain, generously offered up her children, sacrificing for the good of the motherland.

The trinomial connection among the Virgin Mother, motherhood, and motherland in the magazine showed the Basque mother as a source of life, purity, and a figure of sacrifice. In the magazine, the values of the Basque woman/mother resembled the symbolic figure of the Virgin. The mother who sacrificed her children was the salvation of the motherland and therefore its allegorical representation.

The role and image of women in *Euzko-Gogoa* is a unique concept to analyze. It is, however, important to take into consideration the generation of writers and the historical context of the publication. The magazine encouraged the publication of women writers and was positive in creating imagery of the ideal Basque woman. However, although the magazine made space for women, the main goal of promoting this concrete image of the Basque woman was to preserve her traditional role as mother, bearer of the Basque language, helper of her sons, patriotic, Christian, pure, and virginal. This idea of the archetypical Basque women is still strong in the contemporary Basque Country: "Good mother, hard worker and efficient wife."[84] In their patriotic approach, as Mercedes Ugalde states, one of the main missions of Basque nationalist women was to comfort, console, and encourage national reconstruction.[85] Although these women left the house and were able to join "new" spaces, their role was still secondary, very much connected to their role as mother. Although *Euzko-Gogoa* tried to give these women writers their literary and cultural space, the women writers of the magazine and some of the male writers didn't promote women's agency. Subsequent studies in Basque anthropology, such as the one directed by Teresa del Valle's *Mujer vasca imagen y realidad* (Basque Woman, Image and Reality, 1985), will demonstrate the centrality and importance that the mother has had in the ideology of Basque nationalism, both traditional and radical.

The Basque Nation

In the creation of the Basque nation, *Euzko-Gogoa* went back to ancient times to fashion its imagined community. The magazine found its voice in some Basque legends, rebuilding a glorious history, especially in the novels from the end of the nineteenth century, where historical-legendary prose and the costumbrist novel promoted an idealized world. Legendary and historical figures acquired significant value in the reconstruction of the motherland. Aitor, the mythical founder of the Basque people, and Jose Maria Iparragirre, a national poet, became the two main points of reference to portray Basque identity and the Basque nation. They were used to show the deep roots of the Basque Country and to encourage its people to try to emulate their actions in service to Basque national identity.

The references about Aitor appeared in different articles of the magazine. The poem *Euskera maitea* (Beloved Basque Language, 1957), written by Ziriako Andonegi, analyzed the relationship between the Basque language and Aitor:[86]

> Our ancestors left us / the old traditions / the Basque language from where, when, and how / its seeds blossomed. / But through the legend

of Aitor / it was confessed, / explaining that the Basque language is / the language of the Basques / That old Aitor found us / the roots of that language for us, / since then it is ours / sweet Basque language.

Andonegi creates a romanticized idea that the Basque language was a sacred language brought to the Basque by Aitor, a literary character created by the Romantic Basque writer Agustin Chaho (1811–1858). His narrative, *Aïtor - Légende Cantabre* (Aitor, the Cantabrian Legend) was published in 1845 and tells the story of Aitor, the first patriarch of the Basques. As Olaziregi argues, it was the antecedent of this historical-legendary narrative that was cultivated in Spanish by Basque authors in the last third of the nineteenth century and, notably, it influenced the origin of the Basque novel *Auñemendiko lorea* (The Flower of the Pyrenees, 1897).[87]

Coro Rubio, in the book *100 símbolos vascos*, states that Aitor had seven children who populated the seven Basque provinces; it was a clear biblical parallel of the tribes of Israel, expressing a territorial conception of the country that would later be used for Basque nationalism (2016, 42). The legend has biblical connotations; Chaho identifies Aitor with Tubal, the grandson of Noah. Rubio states that since the nineteenth century the Basque language has been defined as *Aitorren hizkuntz zaharra* (The Old Language of Aitor).[88] The Basque language is therefore romanticized as a divine language. *Euzko-Gogoa* published Ziriako Andonegi's poem *Aitorren izkuntz zarra* (1956):[89]

> The language of Aitor / we want to spread, / in front of the world / explain it as men. / If in our veins / there is blood, / The Basques in Basque / should be speaking. / What a beautiful language / our Basque / I can't find anywhere / a better one. / A language with a sweet smell / clean and tidy, / it hasn't got any swear words / a clean speech. / We shouldn't / push aside the language from embarrassment, / less to subjugate it / God gave it to us / for the Basques, / His sacred laws / are not denied / . . . / Our enemies are against us / due to the Basque / since long ago. / Then and now, always / they want to bury it / since long ago, / they are not going to succeed / we will not allow it.

Aitor represented the traditional Basque Country and Basque identity. Andrés Ortiz-Osés states that Aitor is a modern figure who represents the fictional Basque past. Aitor is the personified symbol of the golden age of Basque culture and language (80). The clean and pure Basque language of Aitor was untainted, and it should be spread all over the world. The language reveals the singularity and antiquity of the Basque people.

Jose Maria Iparragirre (1820–1881) was a Carlist ex-combatant and a bard, a traveling singer who sang his songs in Basque throughout different countries of Europe and America. He created the Basque anthem "Gernikako Arbola" (The Tree of Gernika, 1853). In his attempt to recover all the ancestral traditions of the Basques, his work embodied the purest spirit of Romanticism and exhibited an intense Basque patriotism tinged with strong religious connotations. Iparragirre's poems were pillars of Basque nationalist ideology in the following years. Nemesio Etxaniz wrote the poem *Euskal-egazti* (Basque-Bird, 1954), praising Iparragirre and "Gernikako Arbola:

> Let's sing of Iparragirre / poet of the Basque Country: / let's sing to our old country / origin of the best sons: / and the world should listen to / how are we singing, / to the sacred oak we have in Gernika / of our most capable poet. / You weren't born in our country / to be a static tree. / Your heart had the will to walk, / to see the entire world: / dreaming, without peace, / to meet new countries / but in the end you came back to your Motherland / to die.

Nemesio Etxaniz also added to the poem some fragments from "The tree of Gernika / is sacred / among the Basques / loved— / give it and expand it / its fruit in the world / we adore you / sacred tree" (4). The symbol of this tree is one of the most important ones in the Basque Country. It stands for the traditional freedoms of the Basques.

Aitor and Iparragirre both represented ideal nationalists who became a turning point for Basque history and literature. The two showed unique but parallel forms of representing the Basque nation. Aitor, the first Basque, the Basque Adam, embodied the ancient times and deep roots of the Basque Country. Iparragirre, on the other hand, was a universal Basque who sowed the seeds of the Basque language through his songs all over the world.

The rebuilding process of the Basque nation and especially the revitalization of the Basque language were inspired by the modern state of Israel and its process of giving rebirth to Hebrew. Ibiñagabeitia, in an article "Israel" (1952), argued that it was the example to follow in the building process of the Basque nation:[90]

> To you Israel, a new and old country. Bless you. I hope your descendents are as numerous as the sands of the sea! Bring all of your children together; spread out your borders as you did before. The Basques wish you happiness. You will be our inspiration in the hard work we want to do in favor of our unfortunate country. Cheer up Israel.

The rebuilding of Israel in 1948 became for some writers of the magazine an example and an inspiration. In particular, the recovery of the Hebrew language impacted most of the writers for *Euzko-Gogoa*. Antonio M. Labaien stated in the article "Euskeraren kinka gaiztoa:"[91]

> What is happening in Israel should be an example for us, because of that I will give you some examples. Among the news that I have read I will recommend to you the books of Arthur Koestler, because what he wrote about the situation of Israel is well told and explained. It is a true miracle what happened in Israel with the language, as well as what is happening in other fields. But let's focus on the language ... And now, maybe, some of you would ask if we, the Basques, could follow the same pathway. I would answer no. Among us there are many brave people, who, when it was necessary, gave their lives for our country; the ones that are still fighting until death. But our country is totally taken over; we have to admit that we are sloppy in the silent fight for our Motherland. We have the virtue, but we do not take care of the Basque language and teach it at home to our children ...

Emulating Israel was a constant goal for *Euzko-Gogoa*, mainly because of the uniqueness of the process of recovering the Hebrew language. There are few, if any, examples of a language recovery quite like Hebrew. The rebirth of the Hebrew language was a success story, a success that the Basque language would love to have, and that the magazine was trying to encourage.

The magazine portrayed the Basque Country and the Basque people as good and honest people that had its original characteristics from ancient times that were deeply rooted. Among all the distinctive features, the Basque language was the most important one. If the Basque Country lost its language, its essence would be lost. The country would become another country entirely if its language were replaced. This was one of the biggest fears of the magazine. Using the references of Aitor, Iparragirre, and Israel, *Euzko-Gogoa* tried to show its subscribers and the Basque people that they were a unique group that needed to maintain its uniqueness and emulate the path of Israel since the Basques too considered themselves the chosen ones.

In the section "Irakurlearen Txokoa" (Readers Corner) in 1956 in the issue (7–8), the magazine analyzed some African countries in the process of decolonization that began in the 1940s. *Euzko-Gogoa* was glad to announce the end of colonialism, since it represented the configuration of a new historical reality. In fact, one of the consequences of decolonization was independence, something to which many Basques aspired, as published in *Euzko-Gogoa*:

- Each country should have the right to be sovereign, as the priest of Madagascar showed in his letter.

- The new independent country of Ghana is now a free country among others under the sun as of this year. Kwane Nkrumah was the man who helped in the process, and now he is the President. The patriotic footprint of this man is very interesting. The oldest country of Europe, the Basque Country, happily greets the youngest African country. (117)

The magazine saw in the decolonization process a possibility for ending Spanish domination and becoming autonomous and sovereign. The contributors of *Euzko-Gogoa* saw the decolonization movements that were taking place all over the world as a wish and objective for the future Basque nation. If anything, it aroused in its subscribers a desire for independence from Spanish rule.

Ibiñagabeitia wrote to Zaitegi in 1952 that "Iosu Insausti is a Basque writer who escaped from the Spanish Empire."[92] Ibiñagabeitia was aware of the subordination taking place in the Basque Country with the imposition of the Spanish and French language without recognition of the Basque language. In 1959, Bedita Larrakoetxea sent a letter to Zaitegi complaining about the intractable situation of the Basque language and the Basque Country under Franco's dictatorship, and the difficulties in fighting for their rights and identity as Basques:[93]

> In the Basque Country our people are awakening, but Francisco (Franco) came and there is no way to claim any rights. To whom do they have to ask for their rights? He (Franco) is the power, the law. Nevertheless, in our motherland the Basque language is awakening, compared to how things were before, people are learning and writing in Basque.

Larrakoetxea notes that although the Basque language was being revived in the motherland, Franco's dictatorship was still a totalitarian regime. One of the rationales behind the censorship of the Basque language was to obliterate Basque identity, since one of the best ways to eliminate one's identity is to remove one's language. Jorge Oteiza states: "We are a man, with a language and a style. Inside the language is the man and inside the man is the style" (20). Erasing the language removes the capacity to transmit the images, identities, and ideologies of the world contained in one's culture. *Euzko-Gogoa*, in line with the arguments made by Ngũgĩ wa Thiong'o (7), believed that writing and creating in a vernacular language is the main instrument or resistance against an imposition of a foreign language or culture.

Andrés Townsend Ezcurra, the Peruvian writer, politician, and lawyer defined the uniqueness of the magazine in one of its issues:[94]

> The magazine constitutes a singular feat, published in Guatemala, of a purely Basque magazine—"Euzko-Gogoa"—written in the venerable

and vernacular Euskera and under the erudite and skillful leadership of the priest Dr. Joaquín de Zaitegui and Plazaola. The incorruptible fidelity to the Motherland and the aptitude to realize, without boasting, the most disproportionate endeavors. So, in Elcano, in Loyola, in Bolívar, in Lope de Aguirre, in Unamuno. For some reason the only rival of Don Quixote was painted by Cervantes in that courageous "Vizcayan knight" who fought with the Knight of the Woeful Countenance for the most serious combat of all his epic tragicomedy. "Euzko-Gogoa" is the only publication in the world written entirely in Basque. Scrolling through its pages, for the most part, may turn out to be an indecipherable riddle. For those of us who have a cause for affection in our blood, there is a bit of the grandmother's fuzzy tenderness in them, sounds that were heard at some time, in their lap, in the family parish with the missionary in dusty sandals, and irreducible and corresponding effort to revive the memories of the beloved, distant Basque Country.

NATIONAL IDENTITY AND POLITICS IN *EUZKO-GOGOA*
Euzko-Gogoa in many ways attempted to create an image of a nation which alluded to the Basque Country as something unique and special, a romanticized portrait of a country selected by God that was pure in its roots and pure in its language. This country was one rich in history and independent from other influences. The reality of the Basque Country during the twentieth century was very different from the imagined community created in its pages. Zaitegi's goal was to create a cultural magazine that promoted the Basque language and was "free" from politics. However, the reality was that many of the authors and the Basque Country in general underwent years of political turmoil, which influenced the content of the magazine. Inevitably, articles discussed the political situation, attempted to step away from the "imagined," and focused on the "reality." While some contributors of *Euzko-Gogoa* wrote more nostalgic pieces remembering a Basque Country that once was, others were more intent on taking action and regaining their lost country. This section will explore the reality of the Basque communities abroad and at home and the differing ways the various authors discussed their ideal nation, how they would build it, and the obstacles that appeared.

The artistic and cultural production of *Euzko-Gogoa* was used as a promotional strategy to rebuild the defeated Basque Country. *Euzko-Gogoa* was a cultural magazine, but that doesn't mean that it didn't have a recognized ideological canon. *Euzko-Gogoa* was the collaboration of many Basque writers with different opinions, backgrounds, and ideologies. Because of this reality, some of the writers, such as Txillardegi, criticized the political passivity of the magazine since it did not discuss the repression of the Basque people.[95] Too political for some and not enough for others—this was one of *Euzko-Gogoa*'s biggest dilemmas.

Other authors promoted the Aristotelian "golden middle way:" through the broad path of the middle to avoid any political confrontation.[96] Through different works of the magazine, one can recognize the diversity of opinions regarding the "perfect" Basque nation. In this re-creation of the Basque nation, the political inclinations of the writers as well as their generational differences created a gap. Most of the prewar generation of writers believed that the Basque language should be used as a tool to reconstruct the nation. Many writers of the postwar generation were primarily drawn to a more action-based resistance to rebuild the Basque Country. Zaitegi and Ibiñagabeitia, from the prewar generation, wrote:[97]

> The main question of Euzko-Gogoa's generation is the Basque Country, and the salvation of this statement is our language, only the Basque language. The prior generations didn't articulate the Basque Country's question the way we do. They felt the question too, but they didn't see salvation in the language as we do ... There is not any other way: our question will be saved by our language; all the questions of our country must be solved with the Basque language.

The salvation of the country was connected to the use and promotion of the Basque language: the building block to revive the fallen nation, the essential element of what separated themselves from others.

Many of the Basques in exile and in the Basque Country were optimistic that the political reality would be changing after the War of 1936, and the situation would improve. They were hopeful that soon they would be able to return to the Basque Country and resume the lives they had once lived. Unfortunately, the Basque Country did not receive the aid for which they were hoping. Jon Andoni Irazusta, writer and deputy of EAJ-PNV believed that European and North American democracies would save the Basque Country. The article "Beti Bat" (Always One, 1950) demonstrated this Pro-European, pro-ally ideology:[98]

> I firmly believe that this coming war will be won by our supporters, North America and its friends (and if not, may God wait for us). Whether or not this is the case, the liberties of men, families, and peoples will not be ignored, or else men will have lost their very shame. But not; they will not be left in the lurch. When everything is over, the strongest will do everything possible so that freedom prevails, because as long as we do not have freedom we will not be free, since without freedom it has been seen that there is nothing but war ...

According to Leyre Arrieta (2007, 42), the EAJ-PNV began to promote pro-European actions after the First World War: "Indeed, the international situation established after the First World War invited the EAJ-PNV to set its gaze outward."[99] The Basque government aided and fought alongside the Allies in the Second World War hoping they would later assist them with overturning the dictatorship. However, once the Allies won the Second World War, the world turned into a struggle between democratic rule and communism. With the continuing Cold War, the Allies didn't want to overturn Franco to replace him with a Republic and have a communist nation in Europe. As a result, despite the EAJ-PNV actively working with the Allies, its pro-European discourse was delineated and the democracies "turned their back" on the Basques.

Euzko-Gogoa wasn't blind to the reality of the Basque Country. The authors were aware that the world was not going to assist them in their struggle for freedom. As Antonio M. Labaien wrote in the article "Arturo Campion (1854–1954)" in 1954: "In this magazine we shouldn't be talking about politics, but we can't avoid our blood and will, and therefore we bring up in favor of our Motherland and its rights."[100] Many felt that despite their efforts to continue to only promote the language, the situation required more forms of resistance. One can see where *Euzko-Gogoa* not only was a place to create an imagined community but also became a platform where different ideologies coexisted, thus showing the ideological openness of the magazine. These various ideologies allowed for the movement of the imagined community toward a more accurate reality.

The ideology of the necessary steps for change differed among the authors. For some, such as Zaitegi, the ideal form of resistance was through literature. Others felt a more aggressive action-based approach was necessary. Among the authors, Jon Mirande was specific in his call to action. Mirande believed that freedom comes with violence. He criticized the weak democratic spirituality that had prevailed in the Basque Country. He felt that the Basque Country, being a small country, couldn't be free under the European democracies. Joxe Azurmendi (1978, 38) states that Mirande didn't have a middle ground. For Mirande, the Basques had a choice to "be a Christian (democrat) or a patriotic soldier."[101] Mirande was a promoter of violence and a force for the Basque Country to win its place in the world and break with the subjugation. In 1951, Mirande wrote to Zaitegi: "Maybe luck will help us in our pathway toward freedom; the actions in favor of the Basque language without freedom did not bring anything good; however, freedom is not enough."[102]

Through Mirande's poems, *Eresi* (Funeral March, 1951) and *Yeiki Yeiki* (Wake Up Wake Up, 1950), he encouraged Basque youth to fight for their motherland: "Wake up, wake up Basques / all of us friends / all of us friends / to be the masters tomorrow / if we are vassals today / the enemies of our homeland / let's crush them all / let's crush them all."[103] Mirande proposed violence to change the reality of the Basque Country. His article, "Euskaldun gudu-zalduntza baten beharrkiaz" (The Need for a Basque Warbling Cavalry, 1952), was a critique of European democracy and the pro-European politics of the Basque government:[104]

> The majority of Basque-speaking Basques, who want to see their country free and wish to see themselves in their own language, have been in favor of democracy in the last centuries of Europe, with the best ideas: that democratic aspiration is the most obvious symbol of the Basque people, and that the great nations of democracy would win the war (Second World War) and give them the freedom they longed for in the Basque Country. We have seen what has happened to this last point (the situation of the Basques in Spain). Democracies have won the battle, but the Basques who waited for them and fought alongside them are no freer.

He demonstrates his frustration with the lack of assistance from the democratic countries, and for him this requires action.

Mirande's ideology was not independent from other writers, and the atmosphere in the Basque Country began to change. Orixe mentioned in *Euzko-Gogoa* that Basque youth were moving further and further to the left. The first echoes of change were already evident in the magazine. The actions to save the motherland, the sacrifice and martyrdom necessary for the Basque Country appeared in many works. Balendin Aurre-Apraiz's poem, *Deadarra: Guda-osteko gaztediari* (The Call: To the Postwar Youth, 1954), promoted the fight for the Basque Country and showed the patriotic struggle. Aurre-Apraiz was a *gudari* (Basque army soldier) during the War of 1936, was captured by Francoist troops, incarcerated, and exiled. The poem wanted to awaken the youth of the Basque Country to fight for the freedom of their motherland:[105]

> Wake up from your lethargy, child!!! / Don't you hear the sorrow in these mountains? / It is the clamor of lost freedom / They're ours, the howl and the mountains: / Take your weapon and come with us. / There is the outsider trying to destroy us. / Perhaps he does not see the green field covered in blood red? / Your brothers rose up some time ago; / Many have died, many others are still fighting with force.

Juan San Martin, a postwar generation writer, wrote the poem *Aberrimin* (Homesickness, 1956), in which the poetic speaker offered his life to the homeland: "The pathway of freedom / a calvary / Motherland, Motherland! / Take my life."[106] As Benedict Anderson states, the idea of the ultimate sacrifice comes only with an idea of purity through fatality. Dying for one's country, which usually one does not choose, assumes a moral grandeur. Many of the poems like San Martin's had a call for those to take up arms and to take action to take back their country. They created a romanticized and patriotic role that, as Anderson explains, had a sense of purity.[107]

The promotion of violence found a space in the magazine. Koldobika Eleizalde wrote the poem *Izkillu deya* (Weapon Call, 1950):[108]

> Strength; / strength is the highest power / This is what the strangers say / and they want to subjugate us / the Basque Country as a teaching place / Wake up boys! / Answer them back with a weapon! / those of you who want to live in freedom /.../ The moon is up over the mountain / It is the one that shows us the country of our ancestors / If we don't wake up / If we let ourselves die / If we go to our grave in the battlefield / we will die free among weapons / to not see any chain in front of us.

His poem promotes the idea that it was better to die in battle, fighting for the freedom of the motherland, than to live subjugated under the Francoism regime. Continuing with this belligerent tone, Jon Etxaide's play *Amayur* (Amaiur, 1951) represented symbolic references to the history of the Basque Country. Amaiur is a Basque village in the autonomous region of Navarre. In 1521–1522, a group of Navarrese noble men and soldiers entrenched themselves to offer their lives in the last battle while resisting the Kingdom of Castile.

The magazine called for independence. Jon Etxaide wrote the article "Jesus jauna ta San Pedro Euskalerrian barrena" (Jesus and Saint Peter through the Basque Country, 1951):[109]

> Beloved listeners, we are the sons of our ancestors. Let's be their students! Let's allow their unique knowledge to be our mirror! Let's drink the energy of our life from that clean fountain of our ancestors, and not from the dirty water that our enemies are offering us. Because if we drink the water of our ancestors, we will break the chains of subjugation and the Basques will be independent/sovereign.

It is worth mentioning that during this time, these calls for resistance took shape in various forms. The imagined desires of some of the contributors became a reality. Zulaika states that "the resistance kept alive by the PNV was revived by ETA, but ETA's initial stance toward the 'paternal' party was one of rejection. The PNV was seen as a cowardly, conforming father that had done nothing during the twenty years since losing the war."[110]

Zaitegi may not have been very enthusiastic about the ideology of Mirande and others calling for action. Although his idea of resistance was different, he did allow for the publication of their messages. Zaitegi's and other contributors' frustrations with the political situation are quite evident throughout the magazine's existence. Their letters and criticism were an attempt to show those throughout the world the damage that various organizations were doing to the Basque way of life. In a less aggressive form, it was a way to renounce the actions of the Francoist regime and transgressions from other parties.

"THE BASQUE NATIONALIST PARTY WAS THE QUARRY OF PATRIOTISM AS WELL AS THE TOMB OF THE BASQUE LANGUAGE"

Euzko-Gogoa did not openly attack the Francoist regime but was critical of all enemies of the Basque language. The magazine didn't just criticize Spanish institutions like the church and the dictatorship, but it also criticized Basque institutions such as the Basque government (specifically the EAJ-PNV) and Euskaltzaindia (the Royal Academy of Basque Language). Such a critical attitude toward its own people created frictions between the magazine and these Basque entities. *Euzko-Gogoa* always defended the Basque language, and it did not hesitate to reproach the inaction of some Basques who hid behind external factors to not help and support the language enough.

In 1954, Ibiñagabeitia and Zaitegi argued in the "Ataurreko" section (5-8) that the EAJ-PNV's indifference/weakness toward the language impeded/impaired its patriotic spirit.:

> Our people, however, never had the courage to support the Basque language, to speak it, and surrender to it. On the contrary, our people always felt ashamed of it.—It seemed that Basque nationalism would help to open people's eyes. But no ... In our Country the EAJ-PNV was the source of Basque patriotism, but also its tomb. Not with the intention to be that way, but because they did not have any kind of manhood in supporting the Basque language. (74)

The magazine openly castigated the lack of responsibility and sensibility on the part of Basque nationalists and the EAJ-PNV toward the Basque language. Ibiñagabeitia wrote:[III]

> You are asking us how the magazine will survive without the help of EAJ-PNV and Basque nationalists. The help that we have received from them is unfortunately trifling. Between the Basques patriots and members of EAJ-PNV that live in Mexico and Venezuela only five of them paid their annual subscription to the magazine. Despite the indifference of some Basques our magazine is still alive.

Although *Euzko-Gogoa* was not a publication under the control of the Basque government, both Zaitegi and Ibiñagabeitia thought that their work in favor of the language deserved to have the support of said institutions. However, because different events that were happening worldwide, the Basque government did not enjoy economic stability. The relationship between the EAJ-PNV and *Euzko-Gogoa* was weakened over the years. In a letter written by Ibiñagabeitia to Zaitegi in 1959, it is apparent that the Basque government was not at its best:[112]

> The *lehendakari* (Basque president) did not give you any help? It doesn't surprise me. How can he give you any? They barely can maintain the Basque Government. And as you well know, it's better to maintain the Government rather than the Basque language. It's better to feed the Spaniards half-covered with Basque skin than help the Basque language with the nationalist's money.

What Ibiñagabeitia criticized was that the Basque government in exile and Basque nationalists had many avenues to help support the language, but they didn't want to go down those pathways. Without the help and collaboration of the Basque government, many authors saw the future of the Basque language as endangered, because to survive, it needed institutional support. The writer Jon Mix Garai stated in "Euskeraren etorkizuna" (The Future of the Basque Language, 1951): "The government has to strengthen the language; that way the language will be fortified."[113] Although the magazine appeared critical toward the EAJ-PNV or the Basque government, the figurehead and the founder of the Basque Nationalist party, Sabino Arana, was praised. In the magazine, they stated that the pathway created by Arana would be the one they would follow, especially his statements that the Basque Country is their motherland, and that the Basque language is their only language. Ibiñagabeitia, in "Mende-erdi elerti-bidean" (Half of the Century in the Literary Pathway, 1950), wrote of the achievements that the Basque language and literature had realized thanks to Arana:[114]

> The seeds planted by Arana earlier began to flourish in the 1900s. Until that moment, there were not many Basque nationalists in the Basque field. Those few were focused on religious topics and literature. But in order to rebuild a language, in every culture there appears the figure of the poet. In the Basque literary arena, Arana was the first one.

The magazine explained that the revival of Basque literature was the result of Arana. In fact, Ibiñagabeitia in 1958 wrote a letter to Zaitegi, wondering how Arana would have steered through the recent passive attitude toward the Basque language taken by the Basque government in exile:[115]

> If Arana were alive, what direction would he take? Not the one that the Government is taking. His writings are still powerful, and unless we follow his steps we are lost. We are condemned to lose the Basque people along with the Basque Country.

A great deal of nostalgic discourse was in the writings, recalling the days of Sabino Arana when Basque culture was blossoming. The desires to return to those days and to rebuild their nation was evident. In remembering these days of glory, hope, and peace, it was important for some to reflect on what caused them to lose their way of life. With the goal of future nation building, *Euzko-Gogoa* highlighted the necessity of historical memory. It provided a platform to recount the War of 1936, from the voice of the losing side. Mourning the way of life that was lost, remembering what actually took place, and allowing for future generations to know what happened. Memory was used as a form of resistance not only to condemn the atrocities of war, but to discredit the Spanish regime that was still in power.

Balendin Aurre-Apraiz was one of the writers who wrote the most about the War of 1936 and its consequences. His poem *Euzkeltzale batzuen azkena* (The End of Some Basques, 1952) condemns the War of 1936, the Spanish institutions, and the church for the killing of Basques during the war:[116]

> The Spanish police and two priests / another three to help them / thirsty for peace / melancolic mountains; / the good priest / and seven boys / they killed them in jail. / Six men murdering the Basque language / at the edge of the field. / Six men murdering the Basque language / their hands in red blood.

In the short story *Donostiar baten azkena* (The Last of a Native from San Sebastian, 1954), Aurre-Apraiz analyzed the ruthlessness of the victors who were killing Basque people and their freedom, alluding to their dead children and nation:[117]

> The freedom of our Motherland is being broken by our cruel rulers who are killing our sons or daughters. How many people don't know yet where their children are, spread throughout the Basque Country.

Aurre-Apraiz's *Gutun agiria* (Letter Document, 1954) condemned the Catholic Church and its support of Franco: "Our bloody feet in chains, and suppressed in our nation, even if he speaks in the name of the Church, we know who he is, a ruthless bloody dictator."[118]

Not only were there writings condemning actions during wartime, but also during the years of the dictatorship. Writers including Zaitegi and Ibiñagabeitia were opposed to the Spanish regime, referring to it as the "Empire." They worked to show their readers the injustices that were taking place in the Basque Country. Antonio M. Labaien analyzed the difficult years of the dictatorship in his article, "Arturo Campion (1854–1954)": "Later came the dark years 1936–1939, and after the war . . . better if we forget them! Same old thing! Their will is to crush us."[119] He wanted to demonstrate the darkness that followed the war under the Franco dictatorship. *Euzko-Gogoa* not only created an imagined community, but also demonstrated the difficult situation after the War of 1936 and fostered a national consciousness. Reflecting on the prewar years and the years that followed allowed its community to remember their identity and to resist the current state of affairs. The magazine created a foundation of discussion in hopes that one day they would rebuild and return to their ideal nation.

Conclusions

Because *Euzko-Gogoa* has been subjected to minimal prior analysis, this work has a special relevance. The main objectives of this research were to further understand *Euzko-Gogoa*, the imagined community created in its pages, its intrinsic relationship to its historical timeline and events—the War of 1936 and the consequent exile of many Basques—and its impact on the next generation of writers and the path that Basque language and literature took in the 1960s. Ideally, this study will foster new dialogue and questions for future analysis and research about *Euzko-Gogoa*.

The experience of exile creates a unique identity in the individual. In the case of Jokin Zaitegi, his desire to return to the motherland was accompanied by the difficulties of accepting and adapting to new spaces, as was addressed in chapter three. It was in exile that he and other intellectuals rebuilt the foundations of Basque literature, often nostalgically and built on the memory of the motherland. As Federico Álvarez argues, exile makes memories the substitute for permanence, and the exiled abandons the original land, taking with them the one converted into memory. Exile, not being a free choice, carries the burden of keeping alive the old community of feelings (2004, 37).

Although the magazine was innovative, giving the Basque language a space and importance never seen before, it also maintained and promoted certain elements, conditions, and characteristics that resembled the preindustrial Basque Country, such as the ideal Basque archetype described in chapters two and four as an honest Christian Basque speaker. Furthermore, the effects of exile rendered it anachronistic with the reality of the motherland during the 1950s, as explained in chapter four.

The life of exile can go untouched by a true conception of place. As Mercedes Acillona explains, those exiled feel they are in a "lost space" since they are citizens in transit hoping to return to their homeland (81). Therefore, they are living in one place while thinking about another. The separation from the motherland becomes the source of their melancholy and nostalgia, but also the inspiration for their works. For Basques in exile, as has been analyzed in chapter three, *Euzko-Gogoa* created a community of Basque writers and subscribers to feel a connection with their lost country. In this space they could grow and develop the Basque language, nation, and culture all over the world anchored in the traditional and rural Basque Country.

In 1956, Krutwig wrote to Zaitegi: "Zure erebista euskaldun kulturaren hedatzeko bide beharezkoa da, haren gabe orain arte ukhan genuen kanala urik gabe geratuko lirateke" (Kolonia, September 24, 1956. Federiko Krutwig. Gutuneria. KEH-0431-49984. Jokin Zaitegiren Funts Dokumentala. Euskaltzaindiako Azkue Biblioteka eta Artxiboaren dokumentazio bilduma, Euskaltzaindia) [Your magazine is key to promoting Basque culture; without it the rivers would be empty]. The Basque Renaissance that began after the loss of the *fueros* (the old Basque laws) and during the time of *Euskaltzaleak*, an organization formed by some of the best Basque writers of the 1930s to promote the Basque language and honor the culture, created a pathway for Basque language and literature without precedents. After the war, however, the Basque language, culture, and identity were defeated. It was Zaitegi, among others, who, through his magazine, picked up the baton from before the war to give Basque culture a pathway to the future. The promotion of the Basque language was one of the fundamental motives of Zaitegi and the main pillar of the magazine, continuing the previous steps taken before by the prewar authors such as Lizardi and Lauaxeta. *Euzko-Gogoa* was an intellectual magazine and, although its main concern was language and culture, it also made space for political and social concerns.

Euzko-Gogoa wanted to express a "new" literary language promoting the revitalization of a defeated nation, creating a cultural project. For these intellectuals, the normalization and standardization of the language became one of the biggest concerns during *Euzko-Gogoa*'s ten years of publication. Achieving a standardized Basque has been a decisive tool in the modernization of Basque language and culture. The magazine, however, allowed for a discourse among Basque intellectuals to show the necessity of a standardized language for the purpose of academic texts as well as to strengthen the language among its provinces.

In the area of knowledge and cultural growth, *Euzko-Gogoa* created a positive landscape with a commitment to a full set of linguistic capabilities. Pruden Gartzia and Gerardo Markuleta stated in the 1990s that to create an integrated society in the Basque language, you must create a real Basque university, where the Basque language has its own autonomous and monolingual space. *Euzko-Gogoa*, through its translations and works, promoted new fields for the Basque language to build up the Basque literary database to ensure a future for the language. This created a Basque language that was more useful for modern knowledge and creation, an objective that Basque intellectuals strived for especially after the critical situation of the Basque language and culture since the end of the nineteenth century.

The magazine wanted to "renew" and awaken the Basque Country and thus allowed for writers to be the people's guide through the promotion of a "new" Basque language aesthetic. The topics of the magazine created an essential basis for an approach to higher education and advanced studies in the Basque language. For the writers of *Euzko-Gogoa*, the advancement of the Basque Country would have to start with the progression of the language to a higher level. One of the biggest aims of *Euzko-Gogoa* was to develop academic prose through the magazine, which would be suitable for such a future Basque university. Therefore, this magazine was a pioneer in publishing academic and cultured topics at an erudite level of Basque discourse. The idea of having a Basque university was reinforced during the 1930s with the *lehendakari* (Basque president) Agirre. However, it wasn't until 1980, when a Basque public university was officially designated as the University of the Basque Country. Furthermore, the Basque university system, comprised at present of private and public universities from different regions of the Basque Country, has its international counterpart in leading institutions, such as the Center for Basque Studies at the University of Nevada, Reno, the only academic center that offers graduate degrees in Basque studies beyond the borders of the Basque Country.

It is an academic picture that, without any doubt, would not have been possible without the pioneering efforts of institutions and publications such as *Euzko-Gogoa*, a magazine that, as it has been shown, vindicated a cultured language, far from the popular Basque. Its linguistic purism and intellectual style clashed with what was being promoted in the mid 1950s in the Basque Country. The intellectuals in the Southern Basque Country found their new points of reference in Txillardegi, Mitxelena, and Villasante among others, and left behind the language model promoted by *Euzko-Gogoa* or Nikolas Ormaetxea "Orixe." In fact, the varying approaches to the standardization and normalization of the Basque language created an antagonistic relationship between Zaitegi and the influential Mitxelena. *Euzko-Gogoa* promoted a version of the Basque language that was far from the popular use of Basque.

These differing approaches to the Basque language were intrinsically connected to their different realities and backgrounds. Mitxelena, for instance, fought in the War of 1936, was imprisoned twice, and sentenced to death. Mitxelena never sought refuge in exile, and his resistance made him face difficult situations. Furthermore, the academic profiles of Mitxelena and Zaitegi were quite dissimilar, in that Mitxelena had a more profound academic background. Consequently,

I believe that Mitxelena was pragmatic about the reality of the Southern Basque Country under Franco's regime and about Basque language, culture, and politics. He knew this reality from within and could evaluate the transformation and the new needs of Basque society during the crucial years of the 1950s and 1960s. Zaitegi, on the other hand, left the Basque Country when he was in his twenties, leaving him with a much more romanticized vision of his motherland.

When Zaitegi returned to the Southern Basque Country in 1956, his exaggerated and romantic hopes collided with Mitxelena's dry realism. Mitxelena was one of the most important figures of Euskaltzaindia during those years, and Zaitegi's idealism was seen as a threat. Feeling pressured to move to the Northern Basque Country, Zaitegi remained alone without the support for which he was hoping from Euskaltzaindia. Therefore, the normalization of the Basque language was relegated to Mitxelena. Although *Euzko-Gogoa* marked a pathway for many magazines, such as *Egan* (Flying) or *Jakin* (Knowledge), in 1960 it disappeared. However, the Basque literary, cultural, and political "awakening" of the sixties was very much connected to and a result of *Euzko-Gogoa*. The various debates that took place in the magazine regarding the standardization of the Basque language, discussed in chapters three and four, were essential to create the current standard Basque language, *batua*.

In the Basque cultural field, it has been assumed that it wasn't until the origination of *ezker abertzalea* (Leftist Radical Basque Nationalism) and the transformation of EAJ-PNV that the Basque language became the central element of Basque identity. As Fernando Alonso states, in the early years of Basque nationalism, the main emphasis was placed on social and religious factors. However, when the *ezker abertzalea* arrived, it built its foundations on the language (89). This reality created a new scenario for the Basque language in the Southern Basque Country, as described in works such as *Vasconia* (1963) by Federico Krutwig. Krutwig denounces (40–41) and criticizes the conservative and nonrevolutionary politics promoted by the EAJ-PNV. Instead, he promotes a proactive politics and states that the Basque language is the main attribute that personifies the Basque identity:

> The Basque language was the driving force that inspired the Basques to agree upon a feeling of brotherhood that was linked to a community ... The Basque language was the symbol of autonomy and libertarian fraternity ... The Spanish language implied the regime of the exploiter.[120]

The Basque language became one of the main pillars of the new Basque nationalist identity as the cornerstone of thought and the instrument for understanding and seeing the world. Therefore, the language became the tool of politics, culture, and ideology. It was also a unique and unrelated element differentiating the Basque Country from Spain and France.

In the 1960s, the efforts to promote the Basque language increased because of a limited reduction in censorship by the Spanish dictatorship, as shown in chapter three. Furthermore, during the first years of this decade many changes occurred: *Euskaltzaindia* became stronger after the meeting of Baiona (Bayonne) in 1963; standardized Basque language, *euskara batua*, was formed in 1968; Basque language schools, *ikastolas*, re-emerged in the 1960s; and a new Basque musical production began with *Ez Dok Amairu* (The Curse of Number 13 is Broken, 1966–1972). This decade was also important for the awakening of Basque arts with the works of Jorge Oteiza, Nestor Basterretxea, Jose Luis Zumeta, etc. Cultural associations, such as Gerediaga (1965–), were also created. During this decade, Basque literacy campaigns to teach literary Basque were also promoted. These movements' main objective was to recover and revitalize the Basque culture, nation, identity, and language, which were penalized at this time. Consequently, the first step of these cultural-social-political movements was to recover the Basque language and its nationalist role. In the 1960s, a revolution took place in the dissemination of Basque, where the language reached new platforms.

Although the 1960s was a milestone decade, the accomplishments would not have been possible without the seed sown by *Euzko-Gogoa*. After the War of 1936, the magazine exhibited from its very first issue the capacity of the Basque language and manifested how the language was the fundamental pillar for the rebirth of the country, associating the Basque language with nation, identity, and culture. And so I would argue that the relevance of the magazine at such a crucial period as the 1950s has been overshadowed by the improvements made in the ensuing decade. Only researchers such as Iztueta, Intxausti, Aulestia, and Torrealdai have suggested the significance of the 1950s in the development of Basque language and culture.

Euzko-Gogoa tried to evoke and redefine the foundations of the Basque nation, identity, and culture after the War of 1936. The magazine also showed the importance and the necessity of community building by putting together a network of writers and readers from a defeated country to reconstruct it. In this regard, *Euzko-Gogoa* created an imagined community based on traditional Basque nationalism with the ambition of it being the reference for future nation building following the dictatorship.

Through the pages of the magazine the writers created an imagined community that was managed by a group of Basque intellectuals who were envisioning themselves as united, although in different spaces. *Euzko-Gogoa* became a platform that promoted the building of an imagined community founded, as studied in chapter four, upon four pillars: the Basque language being the main one, followed by religion, gender, and nation. However, over time it became clear that the magazine based its imagined community on a dream more than in a reality; it was far from the needs of Basque society at that time. It might be attractive to consider *Euzko-Gogoa* as a utopia since it tried to create and promote an idyllic Basque Country only possible in its pages. However, the drama, desperation, and misery that took place in exile were actually more of an anti-utopian world.

Having both prewar and postwar generation writers with different backgrounds, the magazine became, as described in the chapter three, anachronistic for the goals of the postwar generation of writers, who were moving forward and leaving the past behind. *Euzko-Gogoa* was founded on prewar pillars and ideals that were antagonistic to the reality of the Southern Basque Country in the 1950s. The new generation of writers, Txillardegi, Aresti, Mirande, and San Martin, among others, were much more associated with the new leftist ideology that began to gain relevance among the younger generation in the Basque Country rather than with the Sabinian ideology promoted in the magazine.

This clash with the postwar generation shows the impossibility of success for the magazine since those in exile and those in the Basque Country were moving in two different directions with differing needs, hopes, and desires. *Euzko-Gogoa* was crafted among a community of writers; however, it was the brainchild of Zaitegi. His voice essentially prevailed, and he greatly influenced the imagined community that was created. Also, since it was magazine that was conceived and published in exile, it can be appreciated as a romanticized longing for the motherland that most likely evolved without the presence of those in exile.

The magazine gave voice to women in the intellectual movement of the 1950s. Five women writers, Sorne Unzueta, Karmele Errazti, Julene Azpeitia, Miren Ibargutxi, and Engratzi Iñurrieta, wrote for *Euzko-Gogoa*. They as well as others translated works of women writers such as Selma Lagerlöf, Sister Nivedita, and Gabriela Mistral. Articles were also written about Madame de Staël, Judith, and the Belaustegigoitia sisters (the Caribbean Olympic athletes), as was analyzed in chapter four. The image of women that thrived in the magazine was based on the prewar ideas of Basque womanhood, portraying women as mothers, patriots, virgins, and as metaphors of the Basque motherland.

Marian imagery, as presented in the analysis in chapter four, had a strong influence in the magazine; the Virgin Mary appears as an unattainable ideal of female virtue and as a perfect likeness of a Basque mother. Sacrifice, tradition, purity, and motherhood represent the ideal female figure: a mother who transmitted Basque values to her children and who sacrifices her sons to the motherland to fight for it. This representation of women did not just belong to Basque nationalist discourse, but also to ETA, radical nationalism, as described in studies such as Teresa del Valle's milestone text from 1985.

Through the representation of Basque women, *Euzko-Gogoa* showed in its pages the desired archetypal Basque woman based on those attributes, emphasizing her role as mother and its centrality in the conception of an idealized Basque family. Being rooted in the traditional nationalist ideology, the magazine had women confined to a symbolic role rather than an active one. In this regard, not just the male writers, but also the female writers represented women as domestic agents, as has been shown in the texts of Unzueta, Errazti, and Azpeitia.

Euzko-Gogoa wanted to show that the Basque language was a cultured language and that it could be enhanced to its maximum splendor. As Benedict Anderson asserts, newspapers and magazines are important to promote unification of a national ideology and therefore a sense of belonging as the readers and writers of the magazine become members of a cohesive imagined community. Challenging Francisco Franco's repression of Basque culture and language, the magazine created a platform and became the cultural, transatlantic appeal that provided an imagined community for a defeated nation. This imagined community was based upon the rejection of Spanish rule and the building of the nationalist symbolism forged upon imagery through a vernacular language, community experiences, and collective religious beliefs. In this scenario of exile, this community of Basque intellectuals took the imagery of Basque nationalism and re-created it through literary forms. We have seen that *Euzko-Gogoa*'s idea of a nation was based on literature antagonistic to the claims of Basque society in the 1950s. As a result, after ten years of publication, forty-four issues, 1,171 contributions, 3,658 pages, and the collaboration of 153 writers, the magazine perished. Its Catholic roots, the politics of gender roles, and the static, rural world promoted in its pages were far from what the Basque society was demanding.

Although the magazine ceased publication in 1960, its influence and the work of Zaitegi and its contributors echoed throughout the next generation of Basque literature and culture. The magazine's title, *Euzko-Gogoa,* or "Basque Will" can be symbolic in many ways; the "will" of Zaitegi continued to be present in Basque literary resistance. This "will" demonstrates the accomplishments not only of the magazine but also of the spirit of Zaitegi and the Basques who continued to strive toward the goals of Basque nationhood, identity, culture, and language in the ensuing decades.

Notes

1. My translation.
2. Ibid., 62.
3. Euzko-Gogoa "Opariz" 1950 (1), 3.
4. My translation.
5. "Ataurrekoa" 1954 (1–2), 1. My translation.
6. My translation.
7. "Ataurrekoa" 1954 (1–2), 1. My translation.
8. Ibid., 60. My translation.
9. Ibid., 141–142.
10. "Gure Asmoa" 1950 (2). My translation.
11. Zaitegi, "Euskal-iztegia ta euzkadi'ren berpizkundea" 1952 (1–2), 32. My translation.
12. *Euzko-Gogoa*, "VIII'gn Eusko-Ikaskuntza Batzarraren inguruan" 1954 (3–4), 49. My translation.
13. *Euzko-Gogoa*, "Amilbera" 1954 (5–8), 73. My translation.
14. "Euzkera ezillkorra" 1950 (2), 7. My translation.
15. "Seminario yaunari ongi-etorria" 1952 (7–8), 29.
16. Xemein, "Itz barrijak dirala-ta" 1950 (3–4), 20. My translation.
17. Xemein, "Euzkel-Pizkundia" 1950 (5–6), 6). My translation.
18. "Ataurrekoa" 1954 (1–2), 1). My translation.
19. "Gixadijaren azikera-bidiak" 1950 (11–12), 68). My translation.
20. "Euzko-Gogoa" 1950 (9–10), 35). My translation.
21. Ibid., 33.
22. "Atarikoa" 1957 (9–12), 1. My translation.
23. "Euskal-elertiari buruz" 1951 (7–8), 39. My translation.
24. "Atarikoa" 1957 (9–12), 1. My translation.
25. "1936ko Euskal Unibertsitatearen aurrekariak eta ezaugarriak."
26. Labaien, "Euskeraren batasuna" 1954 (9–10), 154. My translation.
27. Ibiñagabeitia, "Osotasuna" 1952 (11–12), 14. My translation.
28. See Salaburu, *Writing Words. The Unique Case of the Basque Standardization of Basque*. Zaldua, *This Strange and Powerful Language. Eleven Crucial Decisions a Basque Writer is Obligated to Face*.
29. "Krutwig yauna euskeraz" 1950 (11–12), 49. My translation.
30. "Euskal-izkera: Grezitarren itz-etorria" 1954 (5–8), 106.
31. "Aita Mitxelena berrizaleekin" 1952 (1–2), 23.
32. "Eritzi baten eritzia" (1–2), 107. My translation.
33. Xemein, "Itz barrijak dirala-ta" 1950 (3–4), 21. My translation.
34. 1951 (1–2), 11. My translation.
35. Yadarka Yaunari erantzuna" 1951 (3–4), 33. My translation.
36. My translation.
37. Ibid., 139. My translation.
38. My translation.
39. Ibid., 54. My translation.
40. Ibid., 14. My translation.
41. Ibid., 140. My translation.

42   "Atarikoa" 1956 (3–4), 2. My translation.
43   Letter to Zaitegi. Caracas, February 24, 1956. 2.07.01 Gutuneria. KEH-0430-49936. Jokin Zaitegiren Funts Dokumentala. Euskaltzaindiako Azkue Biblioteka eta Artxiboaren dokumentazio bilduma, Euskaltzaindia. My translation.
44   Ibid., 55. My translation.
45   "Xelataka" 1950 (2), 18. My translation.
46   "Atarikoa" 1956 (1-2), 1). My translation.
47   "Euzkera ezilkorra" 1950 (2), 5. My translation.
48   My translation.
49   Ibiñagabeitia, "…Euskera urkatzen" 1954 (11–12), 192. My translation.
50   1955 (3–4), 63. My translation.
51   My translation.
52   Ibid., 133.
53   My translation.
54   Ibid., 52. My translation.
55   Ibid., 11.
56   My translation.
57   Ibid., 12.
58   *The Wretched of the Earth*, 222–223
59   My translation.
60   My translation.
61   (9–10), 36. My translation.
62   Ibid., 101.
63   "Laburrkiro" 25. My translation.
64   Ibid., 181.
65   Ibid., 268–280.
66   Ibid., 16.
67   My translation.
68   Ibid., 293. My translation.
69   "Euzkeraren Alde" 1955 (1–2), 17–18. My translation.
70   (3–4), 52. My translation.
71   Ibid., 646.
72   "Soinez eder, gogoz areago. Judit, biblitar 'pampiresa'" 1957 (3-4), 80. My translation.
73   Ibid., 305.
74   "Gu Euzkadi'rentzat eta Euzkadi Yaungoikoarentzat". (1) 3. My translation.
75   (1–2), 9. My translation.
76   (2), 22. My translation.
77   (1–2), 8. My translation.
78   Ibid., 298.
79   (3–4), 34. My translation.
80   My translation.
81   (1–2), 1. My translation.
82   (3–4), 4. My translation.
83   (11–12), 1. My translation.
84   Bullen, 61.

85 Ibid., 512.
86 (9–12), 3. My translation.
87 Ibid., 18.
88 Ibid., 43.
89 (3–4), 19. My translation.
90 (1–2), 47. My translation.
91 (1–2), 82. My translation.
92 Letter to Zaitegi. Paris, April 3, 1952. 2.07.01 Gutuneria. KEH-0430-49936. Jokin Zaitegiren Funts Dokumentala. Euskaltzaindiako Azkue Biblioteka eta Artxiboaren dokumentazio bilduma, Euskaltzaindia. My translation.
93 Salta, December 22, 1959. 2.07.01 Gutuneria. KEH-0431-49992. Jokin Zaitegiren Funts Dokumentala. Euskaltzaindiako Azkue Biblioteka eta Artxiboaren dokumentazio bilduma, Euskaltzaindia. My translation.
94 "Irakurlearen txokoa" 1950 (2), 31. My translation.
95 Ibid., 46.
96 "Ataurrekoa" 1954 (1–2), 1. My translation.
97 "Etxe aldaketa" 1955 (5–12), 65. My translation.
98 (7–8), 35. My translation.
99 My translation.
100 (11–12), 163. My translation.
101 My translation.
102 *Jokin Zaitigeri egindako gutunak I (1932–1955)*, 241. My translation.
103 "Yeiki Yeiki" (3–4), 7. My translation.
104 (9–10), 18. My translation.
105 (11–12), 166. My translation.
106 (5–6), 4. My translation.
107 Ibid., 144.
108 (5–6), 2. My translation.
109 (5–6), 20. My translation.
110 Ibid., 36.
111 "Irakurlearen txokoa: Eskutitz, galde, iruzkin eta berri" 1954 (11–12), 205. My translation.
112 Caracas, November 12, 1958. 2.07.01 Gutuneria. KEH-0430-49936. Jokin Zaitegiren Funts Dokumentala. Euskaltzaindiako Azkue Biblioteka eta Artxiboaren dokumentazio bilduma, Euskaltzaindia. My translation.
113 (1–2), 12. My translation.
114 (3–4), 8. My translation.
115 Caracas, February 6, 1958. 2.07.01 Gutuneria. KEH-0430-49936. Jokin Zaitegiren Funts Dokumentala. Euskaltzaindiako Azkue Biblioteka eta Artxiboaren dokumentazio bilduma, Euskaltzaindia. My translation.
116 (1–2), 2. My translation.
117 (3–4), 61. My translation.
118 (11–12), 187. My translation.
119 (11–12), 163. My translation.
120 My translation.

Bibliography

Books and Articles

Abellán, José Luis. *El exilio español de 1939 III*. Taurus, 1976a.

———. *El exilio español de 1939 IV*. Taurus, 1976b.

Abellán, José Luis, et al. *Memoria del exilio vasco. Cultura, pensamiento y literatura de los escritores transterrados en 1939*. Biblioteca nueva, 2000.

Acillona, Mercedes. "Espacios en el exilio vasco." Gozález-Allende, Iker. *El exilio vasco*. Deusto, 2016, 79–99.

Agirre, José Antonio. *Escape via Berlin. Eluding Franco in Hitler's Europe*. University of Nevada Press, 1991.

Ahedo, Igor. *The Transformation of National Identity in the Basque Country of France 1789–2006*. Center for Basque Studies. University of Nevada, Reno, 2008.

Aizpuru, Mikel. "50eko hamarkadako abertzaletasuna, jarraipena eta berrikuntza." *Jakin*, no. 159, March-April 2007, 11–33.

———. "1936ko Euskal Unibertsitatearen aurrerkariak eta ezaugarriak." *Zientzia Kaiera*. December 27, 2016. Web. July 5, 2018.

Aldekoa, Iñaki. *Historia de la literatura vasca*. Erein, 2004.

———. *Euskal literaturaren historia*. Erein, 2008.

———. "Gure hirurogeiak." Fernandez, Beatriz, and Pello Salaburu. *Ibon Sarasola, gorazarre: homenatge, homenaje*. Euskal Herriko Uniberstitatea, 2015, 51–63.

Alonso, Fernando. *Por qué luchamos los vasco?* Txalaparta, 2004.

Altube, Belen. *El buen vasco. Génesis de la tradición "Euskaldun Fededun."* Hiria, 2012.

Altuna, Patxi. *José María Estefanía, S. I. (1889–1924) "Maestro de Vascos."* Mensajero, 1990.

Álvarez Arregui, Federico. "Identidad y exilio." Ascunce, José Ángel, and María Luisa San Miguel. *Los hijos del exilio vasco: arraigo o desarraigo*. Saturrarán S. L, 2004, 37–48.

Álvarez, Amaia. "Euskal emakume idazleen lekua literaturaren historian. Dorrearen arrakalak agerian uzten." *Jakin*, no. 148, May–June 2005, 37–75.

Álvarez, José. "La nación imperial. España y su laberinto identitario." *Historia Mexicana*, vol. LIII, no. 2, October-December 2003, 447-468.

Amorrortu, Estibaliz. *Basque Language, Society, Sociolinguistics and Culture*. Center for Basque Studies. University of Nevada, Reno, 2003.

Anderson, Benedict. *Imagined Communities*. Verso, 2006.

Andrés, Ortiz-Osés. *Los mitos vascos. Aproximación hermenéutica*. Univerdidad de Deusto, 2007.

Arana, Sabino. "Somos españoles?" *Bizkaitarra*, no. 4, December 17, 1893, 181.

Arbelbide, Xipri. *Jean Pierre Goytino eta Californiako Eskual Herria*. Euskaltzaindia, 2003.

Aresti, Nerea. "De heroinas viriles a madres de la patria. Las mujeres y el nacionalismo vasco (1893–1937)." *Historia y Política*, no. 31, January-June 2014, 281–308.

Ariznabarreta, Larraitz. *Martin Ugalde: Cartografías de un discurso*. Ekin, 2015.

Ariztimuño, Jose. *Idazlan guztiak 3. Literatura inguruan. Hitzaurreak eta artikuluak*. Erein, 1986.

Arrien, Gregorio. *La generación del exilio*. Gurelan, 1983.

Arrieta, Leyre. "Desde las cunas y los fogones: "Emakume" y emociones en el nacionalismo vasco." Galeote, Geraldine, Maria Llombart and Maitane Ostolaza. *Emoción e identidad nacional: Cataluña y el País Vasco en perspectiva comparada*. Editions Hispaniques, 2015, 197–211.

———. *Estación Europa. La política europeísta del PNV en el exilio (1945–1977)*. Tecnos, 2007.

———. "ETA y la espiral de violencia. Estrategias y víctimas." Rodriguez, Pilar. *Imágenes de la memoria. Víctimas del dolor y la violencia terrorista*. Biblioteca Nueva, 2015, 21–51.

Artetxe, Karmele. "Hizkuntza aferak goi mailako aldizkarietan: Euskera, Euzko-Gogoa, Egan eta Jakin (1921–1960)." *Jakin*, no. 191, July-August 2012, 31–61.

Ascunce, José Ángel, and María Luisa San Miguel. *La cultura del exilio vasco I*. Eusko Jaurlaritza, 1994.

Ascunce, José Ángel. *El exilio: debate para la historia y la cultura*. Saturraran, S. L., 2008.

Atxaga, Mikel. *Euskal emakume idazleak (1908–1936)*. Bidegileak, 1997.

Aulestia, Gorka. "Un siglo de literatura vasca III." *Sancho el Sabio*, no.7, 1997, 13–77.

Azurmendi, Joxe. *Zer dugu Orixeren alde?* Jakin, 1977.

———. *Mirande eta krsitautasuna*. Itxaropena, 1978.

———. *Arana Goiri-ren pentsamentu politikoa*. Hordago, 1979.

———. *Espainolak eta euskaldunak*. Elkar, 1992.

Barandiaran, Miren. *N/A*.

Bazan, Iñaki, et al. *De Tubal a Aitor. Historia de Vasconia*. La esfera de los libros, 2002.

Beltza. *El nacionalismo vasco (de 1876 a 1936)*. Ediciones Mugalde, 1974.

———. *El nacionalismo vasco en el exilio 1937–1960*. Ediciones Mugalde, 1977.

Blot, Jackes. *Artzainak: Les Berges Basques*. Elkar, 1984.

Bullen, Margaret. *Basque Gender Studies*. Center for Basque Studies. University of Nevada, Reno, 2003.

Calleja, Seve. *Haur literatura euskaraz. Lehenengo irakurgaietatik 1986ra arte*. Labayru ikastetxea, 1994.

Cardoza y Aragón, Luis. *La revolución Guatemalteca*. Cuadernos Americanos, 1955.

Chueca, Josu. "Introducción histórica siglo XX." Urquizu, Patrizio, et al. *Historia de la literatura Vasca*. Uned ediciones, 2000, 391–402.

De la Granja, José Luis. *Nacionalismo y II Republica en el Pais Vasco*. Siglo Veintiuno, 1986.

De Pablo, Santiago, et al. *100 Símbolos vascos. Identidad, cultura, nacionalismo*. Tecnos, 2016.

De Pablo, Santiago, Ludger Mess and José Antonio Rodríguez Ranz. *El péndulo patriótico: historia del Partido Nacionalista Vasco*. Crítica, 1999.

Del Valle, Teresa. *Mujer vasca, imagen y realidad*. Anthropos, 1985.

———. *La mujer y la palabra*. Baroja, 1988.

Delgado, Luisa Elena. *La nación singular. Fantasías de la normalidad democrática española (1996–2011)*. Siglo XXI España, 2014.

Diaz, Jon. *Jokin Zaitegiren ekarpenak euskal curriculumean. Eginak eta asmoak*. Utriusque Vasconiae, 2013.

Elorrieta, Joxe. *Renovación sindical. Una aproximación a la trayectoria de ELA.* Txalaparta, 2012.
Etxaniz, Xabier. *Euskal haur eta gazte literaturaren historia.* Pamiela, 1997.
Etxebarria, Igone. *Sorne Unzueta "Utarsus."* Bidegileak, 2000.
Euskal Batzar Orokorra. Eusko Jaurlaritza, 1956.
"Euskal Herriko hezkuntzaren historiarako dokumentazio gunea." *Hezkuntzan Azterketa Historiko eta Konparatuetarako Taldea-Garaian.* Euskal Herriko Unibertsitatea. N/A. Web. October 4, 2017.
Fanon, Frantz. *The Wretched of the Earth.* Grove Press, 2004.
———. *Black Skin, White Masks.* Pluto Press, 2008.
Fraterrigo, Elizabeth. *Playboy and the Making of the Good Life in Modern America.* Oxford, 2009.
Fusi, Juan Pablo. *Política obrera en el País Vasco 1880–1923.* Ediciones Turner, 1975.
Garate, Gotzon. "Lauaxeta Jesusen Lagundian." *Karmel,* no. 224, 2003. 3–23.
Garde, María Luisa. *ELA a través de dos guerras (1936–1946).* Pamiela, 2001.
Gartzia, Pruden and Gerardo Markuleta. "Euskal komunitate zientifiko-intelektuala (eta II)." *Euskaldunon Egunkaria,* May 5, 1994.
Gellner, Ernest. *Nation and Nationalism.* Cornell University Press, 2006.
Gifford, Justin. *Pimping Fictions. African American Crime Literature and the Untold Story of Black Pulp Publishing.* Temple University Press, 2013.
Goikoetxea, Juan Inazio. "Orixe-ren bizi-berri laburra." Ormaetxea, Nikolas. *Euskaldunak poema eta olerki guztiak.* Aunamendi, 1972. Xxvi–xxxvi.
González-Allende, Iker. *El exilio vasco. Estudios en homenaje al profesor José Ángel Ascunce Arrieta.* Deusto, 2016.
Gurruchaga, Ander. *El código nacionalista vasco durante el franquismo.* Anthropos, 1985.
Haritschelhar, Jean. "Literatura ikerketa mende hasieran." *Hegats,* no. 4, June 1991, 9–17.
Hermisilla, Daniela, "I. Judith/Salome." *Daniela Hermosilla.* 2014. Web. 2, March 2018.
Ibarluzea, Miren. *Euskal itzulpengintzaren errepresentazioa euskal literatura garaikidean: eremuaren autonomizazioa, literatur historiografiak eta itzultzaileak fikzioan.* Diss. Euskal Herriko Unibertsitatea. Hizkuntzalaritza eta euskal ikasketa saila, 2017.
Intxausti, Joseba. ""Euzko-Gogoa"-aren lankideak." *Jakin,* no. 12, October–November 1979, 120–137.
———. "Hamar urteko lana (1950–1959)." *Jakin,* no. 13, January–March 1980, 96–119.
———. "Jakin (1956), aurreko eta berehalako testuinguruan." *Jakin,* no. 158, January–February 2007, 53–76.
Irigoien, Alfonso. "Azkue, Arana Goiri eta Unamuno." *Euskera,* no. 33, February 1988, 391–401.
Irujo, Xabier and Alberto Irigoyen. *La hora vasca del Uruguay. Génesis del desarrollo del nacionalismo vasco en Uruguay 1825–1960.* Institución de confrontación vasca. Euskal Erria, 2006.
Irujo, Xabier and Iñigo Urrutia. *A Legal History of the Basque Language (1789–2009).* Eusko Ikaskuntza, 2009.
Irujo, Xabier and Mari Jose Olaziregi. *The International Legacy of the Lehendakari Jose A. Agirre's Government.* Center for Basque Studies. University of Nevada, Reno, 2017.
Irujo, Xabier. *Homo Spelens. Bingen Ametzaga Aresti (1901–1969). Algortar baten bizitza erbestean.* Utriusque Vasconiae, 2009.
———. *Itzulpena erbestean. Bingen Ametzagak Ameriketan euskarara eramandako lanak (1938–1968).* Utriusque Vasconiae, 2009.
———. *Gernika 1937. The Market Day Massacre.* University of Nevada Press, 2015.

Iztueta, Paulo. *Orixe eta bere garaia. V.* Etor, 1991.

———. *Intelligentsia kimatuaren orbelak.* Kutxa fundazioa, 1996.

———. *Erbesteko euskal pentsamendua.* Utriusque Vasconiae, 2001.

———. "Euzko-Gogoa (1950–59): Erbesteko euskaltzaleen lan kolektibo gaitza." Peillen, Txomin. *Euskaldun etorkinak ameriketan.* Utriusque Vasconiae, 2003, 119–134.

———. *Orixe saiogilea.* Utriusque Vasconiae, 2003.

Iztueta, Paulo and Jon Diaz. *Jokin Zaitegi gutunak (1923–1973).* Utriusque Vasconiae, 2007.

———. *Jokin Zaitegiri egindako gutunak I (1932–1955).* Utriusque Vasconiae, 2007.

Jacobson, Matthew Frye. *Special Sorrows. The Diasporic Imagination of Irish, Polish, and Jewish Immigrants in the United States.* Harvard University Press, 1995.

Juaristi, Jon. *El bucle melancólico. Historias de nacionalistas vascos.* Espasa, 1997.

Kintana, Jurgi. *Intelektuala nazioa eraikitzen. R. M. Azkueren pentsaera eta obra.* Euskaltzaindia, 2008.

Kortazar, Jon. *Literatura vasca siglo XX.* Etor, 1990.

Larrañaga, Policarpo. *Emakume Abertzale Batza. La mujer en el nacionalismo vasco.* vol. I. Auñamendi, 1978.

Larronde, Jean-Claude. *El Nacionalismo Vasco su origen y su ideología en la obra de Sabino Arana-Goiri.* Txertoa, 1977.

Lekuona, Aitziber and Iñaki Garrido. *Arbolaren erbesteko sustraiak. Euzkadiko lehenengo Jaurlaritzako burukideen bizitzak.* Herri-Arduralaritzaren Euskal Erakundea, 2006.

Lekuona, Manuel. "La época de Aitzol." Iztueta, Paulo. *Orixe idazlan guztiak VIII.* Eusko Jaurlaritza, 1984, 362.

Lete, Xabier. "Xabier Lizardi, edo poesia gailen." Intxausti, Joseba. *Xabier Lizardi, olerkari eta prosista.* Jakin, 1974, 11–38.

Lizardi, Xabier. *Euskera aundiki-sonekoz.* Klasikoak, 1995.

Llona, Miren. "Polixene Trabudua, historia de vida de una dirigente del nacionalismo vasco en la vizcaya de los años treinta." *Historia Contemporánea,* no. 21, 2000, 459–484.

———. *Entre señorita y garcone. Historia oral de las mujeres bilbaínas de la clase media (1919–1939).* Atenea. Universidad de Málaga, 2002.

Martija, José Antonio. *Eresoinka: embajada cultural vasca 1937–1939.* Servicio Central de Publicaciones, Gobierno Vasco, 1986.

Mess, Ludger. *El profeta pragmático. Aguirre, el primer Lehendakari (1939–1960).* Alga Memoria, 2006.

Mintegi, Laura. *Julene Azpeitia.* Bidegileak, 1987.

Mitxelena, Luis. *Historia de la literatura vasca.* Erein, 1988.

Montaldo, Graciela. "El mundo de la cultura." *Revista Hispánica Moderna,* vol. 64, no. 1, June 2011, 1–9.

Mota, David. *Un sueño americano. El Gobierno Vasco en el exilio y Estados Unidos (1937–1979).* Herri Arduralaritzaren Euskal Erakundea, 2016.

Nuñez-Betelu, Maite. *Género y construcción nacional en las escritoras vascas.* Diss. Faculty of the Graduate School University of Missouri-Columbia, 2001.

Olaziregi, Mari Jose and Lourdes Otaegi. "La representación del bombardeo de Gernika en la literatura vasca." *Revista internacional de estudios vascos,* no. 8, 2011, 40–61.

Olaziregi, Mari Jose. *Basque Literary History.* Center for Basque Studies. University of Nevada, Reno, 2012.

———. "Narrativa vasca del siglo XX: una narrativa con futuro." *Basqueliterature. Portal de literatura vasca.* N/A. Web. September 11, 2017.
Ormaetxea, Nikolas. *Euskal literaturaren historia laburra.* Utriusque Vasconiae, 2002.
Otaegi, Lourdes. "Aitzolen proiektu kulturalaz." *Jakin,* no. 29, October-December 1983, 20–21.
———. *Lizardiren poetika.* Erein, 1994.
———. *Euskera aundiki-sonekoz.* Klasikoak, 1995.
———. *Jon Mirande.* Eusko Jaurlaritza, 2000.
Oteiza, Jorge. *Quousque tandem. ... !* Colección Azkue, 1963.
Preston, Paul. "Las víctimas del Franquismo y los historiadores." Silva, Emilio, et al. *La memoria de los olvidados. Un debate sobre el silencio de la represión franquista.* Ámbito alarife, 2003, 13–21.
Said, Edward W. *Reflections on Exile and other Cultural Essays.* Harvard University Press, 2000.
Salaburu, Pello. *Writing Words. The Unique Case of the Standardization of Basque.* Center for Basque Studies. University of Nevada, Reno, 2015.
Sarasola, Ibon. *Historia social de la literatura vasca.* Akal editor, 1976.
Sarrionandia, Joseba. *Ez gara baitakoak.* Pamiela, 1989.
Smith, Anthony D. *National Identity.* University of Nevada Press, 1992.
Sudupe, Pako. *50eko hamarkadako euskal literatura I.* Utriusque Vasconiae, 2011.
Tabori, Paul. *The Anatomy of Exile: A Semantic and Historical Study.* Harrap, 1972.
Toledo, Ana M. *Domingo Agirre: Euskal eleberriaren sorrera.* Bizkaiko Foru Aldundia, 1989.
Torrealdai, Joan Mari. *Euskal idazleak gaur.* Jakin, 1977.
———. "Euskararen zapalkuntza (1936–1939)." *Jakin,* no. 24, July–September 1982, 5–73.
———. *XX. mendeko euskal liburuen katalogoa (1900–1992).* Gipuzkoako Foru Aldundia, 1993.
———. *El libro negro del euskera.* Ttarttalo, 1998.
———. *La censura de Franco y el tema vasco.* Kutxa gizarte ekintza, 1998.
———. "Yon Etxaide, barne exilioan euskaltzale." *Jakin,* no. 110, January-February 1999, 59–77.
———. "Jakin talde historikoa eta euskara batua." *Jakin,* no. 225, March–April 2018, 11–28.
Txillardegi. *Euskal kulturaren zapalketa.* Elkar, 1984.
Ugalde, Martin. *Unamuno y el vascuence.* Ekin, 1966.
———. "El exilio en la literatura vasca: problemas y consecuencias." Abellán, José Luis. *El exilio español de 1939. VI.* Taurus, 1976, 235–283.
Ugalde, Mercedes. *Mujeres y nacionalismo vasco. Génesis y desarrollo de Emakume Abertzale Batza.* 1906–1936. Euskal Herriko Unibertsitatea, 1993.
Urkizu, Patri. *Exiliatuok ez gara inongoak.* Arabako Foru Aldundia, 1995.
Velez de Mendizabal, Josemari. *Iokin Zaitegi.* Izarra, 1981.
Villasante, Luis. *Historia de la literatura vasca.* Editorial Sendo, 1961.
Wa Thiong'o, Ngũgĩ. *Decolonising the Mind. The Politics of Language in African Literature.* James Currey/Heinemann, 1986.
Woolf, Virginia. *A Room of One's Own.* Harcourt, 1989.
Zabala, Ramon. "Contra el silencio impuesto. Las publicaciones en lengua vasca del exilio de 1936." Gonzalez-Allende, Iker. *El exilio vasco. Estudios en homenaje al profesor José Ángel Ascunce Arrieta.* Deusto, 2016, 99–117.
Zaldua, Iban. *This Strange and Powerful Language. Eleven Crucial Decisions a Basque Writer is Obliged to Face.* Center for Basque Studies. University of Nevada, Reno, 2016.
Zuazo, Koldo. *Euskara batua.* Elkar, 2005.
———. *The Dialects of Basque.* Center for Basque Studies. University of Nevada, Reno, 2013.

Zulaika, Joseba. *Basque Violence*. University of Nevada Press, 1988.

———. *That Old Bilbao Moon*. Center for Basque Studies. University of Nevada, Reno, 2014.

Euzko-Gogoa: Selected Articles

Ametzaga, Bingen. "Adiskidetasuna." *Euzko-Gogoa*, March–June. 1952, 44–49.

———. "LXVI.garren amalaukoa." *Euzko-Gogoa*, November–December 1954, 135.

———. "Plini gaztearen idazkiak." *Euzko-Gogoa*, November–December 1951, 31-32.

———. "Prometeu burdinetan." *Euzko-Gogoa*, January–February 1959, 74–106.

———. "Reading baitegiko leloa." *Euzko-Gogoa*, November–December 1954, 169–172.

Andonegi, Ziriako. "Aitorren izkuntz zarra." *Euzko-Gogoa*, March–April 1956, 19.

———. "Euskera maitea." *Euzko-Gogoa*, September–December 1957, 3–4.

Aresti, Gabriel. "CIXgarren sonetua." *Euzko-Gogoa*, November–December 1954, 164.

———. "Ezer ez." *Euzko-Gogoa*, January–February 1955, 2.

———. "Gauontzak." *Euzko-Gogoa*, November–December 1954, 166.

———. "Ilhargiari." *Euzko-Gogoa*, May–December 1955, 85.

———. "Udazken katua." *Euzko-Gogoa*, November–December 1954, 166.

Argarate, Erraimun. "Euzko-langilleei oyuak." *Euzko-Gogoa*, July–August 1950, 36–40.

———. "Euzko-langilleei oyuak." *Euzko-Gogoa*, September –October 1950, 26–29.

———. "Euzko-langilliei." *Euzko-Gogoa*, January 1950, 23–25.

———. "Euzko-langilliei oyuak." *Euzko-Gogoa*, February 1950, 26.

———. "Euzko-langilliei oyuak." *Euzko-Gogoa*, March–April 1950, 39.

———. "Euzko-langilliei oyuak." *Euzko-Gogoa*, May–June 1950, 50–52.

———. "Euzko-langilliei oyuak." *Euzko-Gogoa*, January–February 1952, 52–55.

Arozena, Andoni. "Xelataka." *Euzko-Gogoa*, February 1950, 18.

Arriandiaga, Imanol. "Cantemus Domino." *Euzko-Gogoa*, May–June 1950, 2–3.

Arrutza, Mikel. "Efeso'ko anderaurena." *Euzko-Gogoa*, January–February 1956, 26–29.

Aurre-Apraiz, Balendin. "Deadarra. Guda osteko gaztediari." *Euzko-Gogoa*, November–December 1954, 166.

———. "Donostiar baten azkena." *Euzko-Gogoa*, March-April 1954, 61–62.

———. "Euskaltzale batzuen azkena." *Euzko-Gogoa*, January–February 1952, 2.

———. "Gaurik gogorrena." *Euzko-Gogoa*, January–February 1952, 1.

———. "Gutun agiria." *Euzko-Gogoa*, November–December 1954, 186–187.

———. "Sortzez garbiari." *Euzko-Gogoa*, November–December 1951, 1.

Azpeitia, Julene. "Goizeko izarra." *Euzko-Gogoa*, January–February 1959, 61–65.

Egaña, Gotzon. "Soiñez eder, gogoz areago. Judit, biblitar pampiresa." *Euzko-Gogoa*, March–April 1957, 80–83.

Eleizalde, Koldo. "Izkillu deya." *Euzko-Gogoa*, May–June 1950, 2.

Erkiaga, Eusebio. "Bei itsua." *Euzko-Gogoa*, March–April 1958, 123.

Errazti, Karmele. "Euzko-Gogoa." *Euzko-Gogoa*, September–October 1950, 36.

———. "Juan yakuzan bixitz oroigarrijak." *Euzko-Gogoa*, September–October 1951, 55–56.

Errexil. "'Euzko-Gogoa-'ri buruz." *Euzko-Gogoa*, February 1950, 22.

Etxaide, Jon. "Amayur." *Euzko-Gogoa*, January–February 1951, 20–24.

———. "Amayur." *Euzko-Gogoa*, March–April 1951, 38–43.

———. "Amayur." *Euzko-Gogoa*, May–June 1951, 21–25.

———. "Amayur." *Euzko-Gogoa*, July–August 1951, 18–27.

———. "Amayur." *Euzko-Gogoa*, September–October 1951, 30–34.
———. "Arangio'ko basalorea." *Euzko-Gogoa*, September–October 1952, 7–9.
———. "Euskal-elertia prantziskotarren kantauri barruan (1)." *Euzko-Gogoa*, November–December 1954, 174–178.
———. "Jesus jauna ta San Pedro Euskalerrian barrena." *Euzko-Gogoa*, May–June 1951, 14–20.
Etxaniz, Nemesio. "Ama!" *Euzko-Gogoa*, January–February 1952, 8.
———. "Euskal-egazti." *Euzko-Gogoa*, January–February 1954, 4–8.
———. "Maitasun ixilla." *Euzko-Gogoa*, May–June 1956, 63–67.
———. "Tellagorri." *Euzko-Gogoa*, July–August 1957, 57–62.
Etxeberria, Frantzisko. "Dabid'en eresiak XLVII-garrena." *Euzko-Gogoa*, March–April 1957, 6–7.
———. "Dabid'en eresiak XVII." *Euzko-Gogoa*, March–April 1957, 4–5.
Euzko-Gogoa. "Amerika-Erdi ta Karibe'ko VI'garren Olinpiar Yolasak." *Euzko-Gogoa*, March–April 1950, 52–53.
———. "Atarikoa." *Euzko-Gogoa*, September–December 1957, 1.
———. "Atarikoa." *Euzko-Gogoa*, March–April 1956, 1–2.
———. "Atarikoa." *Euzko-Gogoa*, January–February 1956, 1–3.
———. "Atarikoa." *Euzko-Gogoa*, May–June 1956, 1–2.
———. "Atarikoa." *Euzko-Gogoa*, July–August 1956, 1–2.
———. "Atarikoa." *Euzko-Gogoa*, May–June 1957, 1–2.
———. "Atarikoa." *Euzko-Gogoa*, July–August 1957, 1.
———. "Atarikoa." *Euzko-Gogoa*, January–February 1958, 1–2.
———. "Atarikoa." *Euzko-Gogoa*, March–April 1957, 121.
———. "Atarikoa." *Euzko-Gogoa*, May–August 1958, 241–242.
———. "Atarikoa." *Euzko-Gogoa*, September–December 1958, 437.
———. "Atarikoa." *Euzko-Gogoa*, January–February 1958, 1–2.
———. "Atarikoa." *Euzko-Gogoa*, March–June 1959, 121–122.
———. "Ataurrekoa." *Euzko-Gogoa*, January–February 1954, 1.
———. "Ataurrekoa." *Euzko-Gogoa*, March–April 1954, 49.
———. "Ataurrekoa." *Euzko-Gogoa*, September–October 1954, 131–132.
———. "Ataurrekoa. Amilbera." *Euzko-Gogoa*, May–August 1954, 73–74.
———. "Etxe-aldaketa." *Euzko-Gogoa*, May–December 1955, 65.
———. "Eup! Euzko-Gogoaren arpidedunei!" *Euzko-Gogoa*, July–August 1951, 27.
———. "Euskera ta Euzko-Gogoa." *Euzko-Gogoa*, May–June 1956, 1–2.
———. "Euskera ta Euzko-Gogoa." *Euzko-Gogoa*, May–June 1956, 1–2.
———. "Euzko-Gogoa." *Euzko-Gogoa*, July–August 1951, 60.
———. "Irakurlearen txokoa." *Euzko-Gogoa*, February 1950, 31.
———. "Irakurlearen txokoa." *Euzko-Gogoa*, July–August 1956, 116–120.
———. "Irakurlearen txokoa." *Euzko-Gogoa*, January–February 1954, 47–48.
———. "Irakurlearen txokoa." *Euzko-Gogoa*, March–April 1954, 68–69.
———. "Irakurlearen txokoa." *Euzko-Gogoa*, May–August 1954, 123–125.
———. "Irakurlearen txokoa." *Euzko-Gogoa* September–October 1954, 159–160.
———. "Irakurlearen txokoa." *Euzko-Gogoa*, March–April 1955, 62–64.
———. "Irakurlearen txokoa." *Euzko-Gogoa*, May–December 1955, 139–141.
———. "Irakurlearen txokoa." *Euzko-Gogoa*, May–June 1956, 115–120.

———. "Irakurlearen txokoa." *Euzko-Gogoa*, June–December 1956, 11–120.
———. "Irakurlearen txokoa." *Euzko-Gogoa*, September–October 1956, 114–120.
———. "Irakurlearen txokoa." *Euzko-Gogoa*, November–September 1956, 117–120.
———. "Irakurlearen txokoa." *Euzko-Gogoa*, January –February 1957, 116–120.
———. "Irakurlearen txokoa." *Euzko-Gogoa*, March–April 1957, 117–120.
———. "Irakurlearen txokoa." *Euzko-Gogoa*, May–June 1957, 117–120.
———. "Irakurlearen txokoa." *Euzko-Gogoa*, July–August 1957, 118–120.
———. "Irakurlearen txokoa." *Euzko-Gogoa*, September–December 1957, 187–192.
———. "Irakurlearen txokoa." *Euzko-Gogoa*, January–February 1958, 117–120.
———. "Irakurlearen txokoa." *Euzko-Gogoa*, September–December 1958, 702–706.
———. "Irakurlearen txokoa." *Euzko-Gogoa*, January–February 1959, 117–120.
———. "Irakurlearen txokoa." *Euzko-Gogoa*, March–April 1955, 62–64.
———. "Irakurlearen txokoa." *Euzko-Gogoa*, January–February 1956, 116–120.
———. "Iraurlearen txokoa." *Euzko-Gogoa*, November–December 1954, 205–207.
———. "VIII'gn. Eusko-Ikaskuntza-Batzarraren inguran. Asmoz ta Jakitez bai, banan EUSKERAZ." *Euzko-Gogoa*, March–April 1954, 49.
G.E.A. "Begoñako Ama neskutz bizkaitarren zaindarija." *Euzko-Gogoa*, March–April 1952, 4.
Garai, Jon Mix. "Euskeraren etorkizuna." *Euzko-Gogoa*, January–February 1951, 12.
Garate, Gotzon. "Europako erri zaarena. Euskaldunen izkuntza, lantze eta oituretzaz." *Euzko-Gogoa*, January–February 1959, 34–38.
Ibargutxi, Miren Arrate. "Bakarrik, negarrez, zoriontsu." *Euzko-Gogoa*, September –December 1958, 447.
———. "Euskal-Erriko mendietan." *Euzko-Gogoa*, January–February 1959, 18.
———. "Zaude lo, kutuna." *Euzko-Gogoa*, January–February 1959, 19.
Ibiñagabeitia, Andima. " . . . Euskera urkatzen!" *Euzko-Gogoa*, November–December 1954, 191–193.
———. "Aldizkariak." *Euzko-Gogoa*, September–October 1954, 162.
———. "Aldizkariak." *Euzko-Gogoa*, November–December 1954, 209.
———. "Aldizkariak barna." *Euzko-Gogoa*, September–October 1951, 66–68.
———. "Aldizkariak-barna." *Euzko-Gogoa*, May–June 1952, 25–29.
———. "Bergil'ren unai-kantak (Bukolikoak)." *Euzko-Gogoa*, November–December 1954, 178–179.
———. "Bergili'ren Unai-Kantak (Bukolikoak)." *Euzko-Gogoa*, January–February 1955, 11–12.
———. "Bergili'ren Unai-Kantak (Bukolikoak)." *Euzko-Gogoa*, March–April 1955, 47–49.
———. "Erleak eta heriotza." *Euzko-Gogoa*, May–August 1954, 122–123.
———. "Etxe aldaketa." *Euzko-Gogoa*, June–December 1955, 65.
———. "Euskal mitologiaren ikaspiderako." *Euzko-Gogoa*, September–October 1954, 155–158.
———. "Euskal mitologiaren ikaspiderako." *Euzko-Gogoa*, January–February 1955, 23–25.
———. "Euzko-Gogoa." *Euzko-Gogoa*, September–October 1950, 33–36.
———. "Israel." *Euzko-Gogoa*, January–February 1952, 46–47.
———. "Maitasun eta erio kanta." *Euzko-Gogoa*, January–February 1957, 56–72.
———. "Mende-erdi elerti-bidean." *Euzko-Gogoa*, March–April 1950, 8–10.
———. "Osotasuna." *Euzko-Gogoa*, November–December 1952, 12–14.
Insausti, Jesus. "Antzinako maitasun-edesti bat." *Euzko-Gogoa*, January–February 1955, 6–8.
———. "Gau donea." *Euzko-Gogoa*, March–April 1954, 56–57.
———. "Hanfor'erako ibillaldia." *Euzko-Gogoa*, September–October 1952, 9–12.

———. "Ibillaldietarako oarrak." *Euzko-Gogoa*, September–October 1954, 136.
———. "Neskazarra." *Euzko-Gogoa*, May–December 1955, 95–99.
———. "Zaldi zuriaren edestia." *Euzko-Gogoa*, March–April 1952, 32–35.
Iñurrieta, Engratzi. "Kartzelakoa'ren ongi-etorria." *Euzko-Gogoa*, May–June 1956, 11.
Irazusta, Jon Andoni. "Beti bat." *Euzko-Gogoa*, July–August 1950, 35.
Irigoien, Alfonso. "Gaitzetsia." *Euzko-Gogoa*, November–December 1954, 196–197.
Iturrioz, Antonio. "Alzateko jauna." *Euzko-Gogoa*, May–December 1955, 94–95.
Jauregi, A. "Arrigorria'ko guda." *Euzko-Gogoa*, November–December 1956, 43–49.
Jauregi, Migel. "Adiskide zintzoa." *Euzko-Gogoa*, January–February 1959, 48–60.
Jautarkol. "Anai-arteko gudatean." *Euzko-Gogoa*, January–February 1952, 9.
Kerexeta, Jaime. "Euzkeraren alde." *Euzko-Gogoa*, January–February 1955, 17–18.
Krutwig, Federiko. "Seminario yaunari ongi-etorria." *Euzko-Gogoa*, June–August 1952, 29–31.
Labaien, Antonio M. "Arturo Campion (1854–1954)." *Euzko-Gogoa*, November–December 1954, 163.
———. "Euskeraren batasuna." *Euzko-Gogoa*, September–October 1954, 154–155.
———. "Euskeraren kinka gaiztoa." *Euzko-Gogoa*, January–February 1958, 74–80.
———. "Linkeus dorrezaia." *Euzko-Gogoa*, September–October 1951, 6.
Larrakoetxea, Bedita. "Ekatxa." *Euzko-Gogoa*, March–June 1959, 171–245.
———. "Lear errege." *Euzko-Gogoa*, May–June 1958, 243–372.
———. "Macbeth." *Euzko-Gogoa*, September–December 1957, 58–131.
Larrañaga, Eladio. "Lear Erregea." *Euzko-Gogoa*, March–April 1951, 20–27.
———. "Neguko ipuina." *Euzko-Gogoa*, November–December 1950, 5–6.
Larrañaga, Gillermo. "Izkuntza eta abenda." *Euzko-Gogoa*, January–February 1959, 23–25.
———. "Mila ta bat gauetako ipuiak." *Euzko-Gogoa*, July–August 1956, 42–51.
———. "Mila ta bat gauetako ipuinak (iarraipena)." *Euzko-Gogoa*, January–February 1957, 37–43.
———. "Milla ta bat gauetako ipuinak (iarraipena)." *Euzko-Gogoa*, March–April 1958, 181–195.
Mirande, Jon. "Akelarre." *Euzko-Gogoa*, March–April 1950, 7.
———. "Amontillado Upela." *Euzko-Gogoa*, July–August 1952, 21–23.
———. "Ba-nin adiskide bat." *Euzko-Gogoa*, May–June 1950, 5.
———. "Beiak." *Euzko-Gogoa*, September–October 1951, 9.
———. "Bela." *Euzko-Gogoa*, September–October 1950, 5–6.
———. "Bi beleak." *Euzko-Gogoa*, March–April 1950, 7.
———. "Bi fraideak." *Euzko-Gogoa*, January–February 1956, 89–94.
———. "Breiziera." *Euzko-Gogoa*, September–October 1951, 9.
———. "Burua." *Euzko-Gogoa*, January–February 1957, 49–53.
———. "Eresi." *Euzko-Gogoa*, September–October 1951, 4.
———. "Eros arrosen artean." *Euzko-Gogoa*, May–August 1954, 76.
———. "Euskaldun gudu-zalduntza baten beharrkiaz." *Euzko-Gogoa*, September–October 1952, 18–19.
———. "Goiztar txoriek kanta bezate." *Euzko-Gogoa*, May–June 1951, 5–6.
———. "Ixiltze." *Euzko-Gogoa*, March–April 1951, 6–8.
———. "La Belle Dame sans merci." *Euzko-Gogoa*, March–April 1952, 5.
———. "Legearen aitzinean." *Euzko-Gogoa*, January–Feburary 1954, 21–22.
———. "Lekhoreko biziarena." *Euzko-Gogoa*, January–February 1954, 10.

———. "Lotazillak amabi." *Euzko-Gogoa*, Noember–December 1950, 2.
———. "Ortzi'ren ttunttuna." *Euzko-Gogoa*, November–December 1952, 2.
———. "Yeiki yeiki." *Euzko-Gogoa*, March–April 1950, 7.
———. "Zaldiz zeruan." *Euzko-Gogoa* January–February 1957, 6.
Mitxelena, Salbatore. "Guruz bidea. Euskal samiñarena." *Euzko-Gogoa*, March–April 1955, 34–36.
Mokoroa, Justo M. "Erraondoko azken danbolinteroa." *Euzko-Gogoa*, September–October 1952, 13–14.
———. "Erraondo'ko danbolinteroa (Iarraipena)." *Euzko-Gogoa*, March–April 1955, 40–42.
Mujika, Luis Mari. "Pinotxo'ren biurrikeriak." *Euzko-Gogoa*, January–February 1959, 66–73.
N/A. "El INFOP, Esperanza de Guatemala." *Euzko-Gogoa*, March–April 1950, 2.
———. "Hacia el futuro agrario." *Euzko-Gogoa*, January–February 1954, 49.
Oiartzabal, Martin. "Aosta'ko legenarduna." *Euzko-Gogoa*, March–June 1959, 155–170.
———. "Ianko ereslari." *Euzko-Gogoa*, January–February 1957, 44–48.
Onaindia, Santi. "Enea'rena." *Euzko-Gogoa*, July–August 1956, 111–115.
———. "Enea'rena." *Euzko-Gogoa*, May–June 1957, 100–105.
Ormaetxea, Nikolas and Martin Oiartzabal. "Euskal-izkera: Grezitarren itz-etorria." *Euzko-Gogoa*, May–August 1954, 106.
Ormaetxea, Nikolas. "Erria, erria! Berriz eta azkenekoz." *Euzko-Gogoa*, January–February 1951, 10–12.
———. "Kito'n arrebarekin." *Euzko-Gogoa*, September–October 1951, 20–29.
———. "Aita Mitxelena berrizaleekin." *Euzko-Gogoa*, January–February 1952, 23–25.
———. "Kito'n arrebarekin." *Euzko-Gogoa*, May-June 1952, 14–18.
———. "Kito'n arrebarekin." *Euzko-Gogoa*, July–August 1952, 10–16.
———. "Kito'n arrebarekin." *Euzko-Gogoa*, November–December 1952, 23–27.
———. "Kito'n arrebarekin." *Euzko-Gogoa*, January–February 1954, 12–15.
———. "Kito'n arrebarekin." *Euzko-Gogoa*, March–April 1954, 58–61.
———. "Kito'n arrebarekin." *Euzko-Gogoa*, May-August 1954, 87–90.
———. "Krutwig yaunari euskeraz." *Euzko-Gogoa*, November–December 1950, 49–52.
———. "Quito'n arrebarekin." *Euzko-Gogoa*, November–December 1950, 12–15.
———. "Quito'n arrebarekin." *Euzko-Gogoa*, March–April 1951, 13–19.
———. "Quito'n arrebarekin." *Euzko-Gogoa*, May–June 1951, 7–10.
———. "Quito'n arrebarekin." *Euzko-Gogoa*, July–August 1951, 39–47.
San Martin, Juan. "Aberrimin." *Euzko-Gogoa*, May–June 1956, 4.
———. "Eritzi baten eritzia." *Euzko-Gogoa*, January–February 1957, 106–110.
———. "Zeun nai duzuna." *Euzko-Gogoa*, March–June 1959, 130.
Sorrarain, Antonio. "Itzaltzuko koblaria." *Euzko-Gogoa*, May–August 1954, 81–85.
Tauer, Norbert. "Euskal-elertiari buruz." *Euzko-Gogoa*, July–August 1951, 38–39.
Unzueta, Sorne. "Artxanda." *Euzko-Gogoa*, March–April 1952, 4.
———. "Itxartu, euzko-alabea." *Euzko-Gogoa*, September–October 1950, 15–16.
Urrutia, Gotzon. "Euzkera ezilkorra." *Euzko-Gogoa*, February 1950, 5–7.
———. "Gixadijaren azikera-bidiak." *Euzko-Gogoa*, November–December 1950, 65–68.
Xemein, Keperin. "Euzkel-Pizkundia." *Euzko-Gogoa*, May-June 1950, 6–7.
———. "Itz barrijak dirala-ta." *Euzko-Gogoa*, March–April 1950, 22.
———. "Laburrkiro." *Euzko-Gogoa*, March–April 1952, 25.

Zaitegi, Jokin. "Aiatz." *Euzko-Gogoa*, May–June 1957, 12–35.
———. "Aitzol'en gizaldia." *Euzko-Gogoa*, January 1950, 7.
Zaitegi, Jokin and Andima Ibinagabeitia. "Abere-indarra." *Euzko-Gogoa*, March-April 1950, 11–19.
———. "Abere-indarra." *Euzko-Gogoa*, May–June 1950, 27–35.
Zaitegi, Jokin. "Angelus." *Euzko-Gogoa*, March–April 1952, 54–55.
———. "Arroteztxeko alaba." *Euzko-Gogoa*, May–June 1951, 5.
———. "Begiak." *Euzko-Gogoa*, September–October 1952, 2.
———. "Bi gogoen eresia." *Euzko-Gogoa*, May–June 1951, 4.
———. "Epail eguna." *Euzko-Gogoa*, January–February 1951, 4.
———. "Erbestean aritza." *Euzko-Gogoa*, November–December 1952, 1.
———. "Euskal-Iztegia'ren berpizkundea." *Euzko-Gogoa*, January–February 1952, 32–34.
———. "Fomentor'ko lerrondoa." *Euzko-Gogoa*, September–October 1950, 4–5.
———. "Goiz-eresia." *Euzko-Gogoa*, January–February 1951, 5.
———. "Gure asmoa." *Euzko-Gogoa*, February 1950, p. Azal barnea.
———. "Irukoitza." *Euzko-Gogoa*, September–October 1950, 4.
———. "Mari Beltxa." *Euzko-Gogoa*, September–October 1952, 6–7.
———. "Nere atsekabe aundi." *Euzko-Gogoa*, January–February 1951, 5.
———. "Neska zapuztua." *Euzko-Gogoa*, January–February 1951, 4.
———. "Opariz." *Euzko-Gogoa*, January 1950, 3.
———. "Orixe'ren Euskaldunak." *Euzko-Gogoa*, July-August 1950, 12.
———. "Piloktete." *Euzko-Gogoa*, September–December 1957, 12–57.
———. "Sinisten dut askatasunean." *Euzko-Gogoa*, November–December 1956, 28–42.
———. "Stael anderea (1766–1817)." *Euzko-Gogoa*, May–June 1951, 11–13.
———. "Tarakin'go emaztekiak." *Euzko-Gogoa*, July–August 1957, 12–52.
———. "Umezurtz." *Euzko-Gogoa*, January–Febuary 1959, 22.
———. "Yadarka Yaunari erantzuna." *Euzko-Gogoa*, March–April 1951, 33–34.
Zatarain, Anbrosio. "Balekiye." *Euzko-Gogoa*, July–August 1950, 3.
Zinkunegi, Joseba. "Kepa deunaren ollaskoa." *Euzko-Gogoa*, September-October 1956, 54–56.
———. "Kozko-muñoa." *Euzko-Gogoa*, March-April 1958, 173–180.

Archival Collections

Agirre, José Antonio. Letter to Jokin Zaitegi. Paris, November 15, 1951. 2.07.01 Gutuneria. KEH-0427-49693. Jokin Zaitegiren Funts Dokumentala. Euskaltzaindiako Azkue Biblioteka eta Artxiboaren dokumentazio bilduma, Euskaltzaindia, Bilbao, Basque Country, SP. November 14, 2016.

Ibiñagabeitia, Andima. Letter to Jon Mirande. Paris, August 28, 1951. 2.02.4. AIB. KEH-0152. Box 012, File 001. Andima Ibiñagabeitiaren Funts Dokumentala. Euskaltzaindiako Azkue Biblioteka eta Artxiboaren dokumentazio bilduma, Euskaltzaindia, Bilbao, Basque Country, SP. October 5, 2016.

Ibiñagabeitia, Andima. Letter to Zaitegi. Paris, April 25, 1951. 2.07.01 Gutuneria. KEH-0430-49936. Jokin Zaitegiren Funts Dokumentala. Euskaltzaindiako Azkue Biblioteka eta Artxiboaren dokumentazio bilduma, Euskaltzaindia, Bilbao, Basque Country, SP. October 20, 2016.

———. Letter to Zaitegi. Paris, April 3, 1952. 2.07.01 Gutuneria. KEH-0430-49936. Jokin Zaitegiren Funts Dokumentala. Euskaltzaindiako Azkue Biblioteka eta Artxiboaren dokumentazio bilduma, Euskaltzaindia, Bilbao, Basque Country, SP. October 20, 2016.

———. Letter to Zaitegi. Caracas, February 24, 1956. 2.07.01 Gutuneria. KEH-0430-49936. Jokin Zaitegiren Funts Dokumentala. Euskaltzaindiako Azkue Biblioteka eta Artxiboaren dokumentazio bilduma, Euskaltzaindia, Bilbao, Basque Country, SP. October 20, 2016.

———. Letter to Zaitegi. Kolonia, September 24, 1956. Federiko Krutwig. Gutuneria. KEH-0431-49984. Jokin Zaitegiren Funts Dokumentala. Euskaltzaindiako Azkue Biblioteka eta Artxiboaren dokumentazio bilduma, Euskaltzaindia, Bilbao, Basque Country, SP. October 20, 2016.

———. Letter to Zaitegi. Caracas, February 6, 1958. 2.07.01 Gutuneria. KEH-0430-49936. Jokin Zaitegiren Funts Dokumentala. Euskaltzaindiako Azkue Biblioteka eta Artxiboaren dokumentazio bilduma, Euskaltzaindia, Bilbao, Basque Country, SP. October 20, 2016.

———. Letter to Zaitegi. Larrakoetxea, Bedita. Salta, December 22, 1959. 2.07.01 Gutuneria. KEH-0431-49992. Jokin Zaitegiren Funts Dokumentala. Euskaltzaindiako Azkue Biblioteka eta Artxiboaren dokumentazio bilduma, Euskaltzaindia, Bilbao, Basque Country, SP. November 17, 2016.

———. Letter to Zaitegi. Caracas, November 12, 1959. 2.07.01 Gutuneria. KEH-0430-49936. Jokin Zaitegiren Funts Dokumentala. Euskaltzaindiako Azkue Biblioteka eta Artxiboaren dokumentazio bilduma, Euskaltzaindia, Bilbao, Basque Country, SP. October 20, 2016.

Zaitegi, Jokin. Letter to Pablo Gurpide. Bilbao, April 10, 1956. 2.07.01 Gutuneria. KEH-0430-49916. Jokin Zaitegiren Funts Dokumentala. Euskaltzaindiako Azkue Biblioteka eta Artxiboaren dokumentazio bilduma, Euskaltzaindia, Bilbao, Basque Country, SP. October 20, 2016.

———. Letter to José Ibañez. Bilbao, May 7, 1956. 2.07.01 Gutuneria. KEH-0430-49931. Jokin Zaitegiren Funts Dokumentala. Euskaltzaindiako Azkue Biblioteka eta Artxiboaren dokumentazio bilduma, Euskaltzaindia, Bilbao, Basque Country, SP. October 20, 2016.

———. Letter to Antonio Tovar. Guatemala, August 13, 1955. 2.07.01 Gutuneria. KEH-0433-50137. Jokin Zaitegiren Funts Dokumentala. Euskaltzaindiako Azkue Biblioteka eta Artxiboaren dokumentazio bilduma, Euskaltzaindia, Bilbao, Basque Country, SP. October 20, 2016.

Zaitegi, Jokin. Letter to Andima Ibiñagabeitia. Guatemala, February 23, 1953. 2.02.1. AIB. KEH-0146. Box 006, File 242. Andima Ibiñagabeitiaren Funts Dokumentala. Euskaltzaindiako Azkue Biblioteka eta Artxiboaren dokumentazio bilduma, Euskaltzaindia, Bilbao, Basque Country, SP. October 5, 2016.

———. Letter to Andima Ibiñagabeitia. Miarritze, September 25, 1957. 2.02.1. AIB. KEH-0146. Box 006, File 242. Andima Ibiñagabeitiaren Funts Dokumentala. Euskaltzaindiako Azkue Biblioteka eta Artxiboaren dokumentazio bilduma, Euskaltzaindia, Bilbao, Basque Country, SP. October 5, 2016.

———. Letter to Andima Ibiñagabeitia. Miarritze, December 20, 1957. 2.02.1. AIB. KEH-0146. Box 006, File 242. Andima Ibiñagabeitiaren Funts Dokumentala. Euskaltzaindiako Azkue Biblioteka eta Artxiboaren dokumentazio bilduma, Euskaltzaindia, Bilbao, Basque Country, SP. November 13, 2016.

Zaitegi, Jokin. Agreement 4.42 "Guridi Jaunak esana" File 360-001. First Basque World Congress. Borrador de parte de los debates tenidos por la sección de Cultura del Congreso Mundial Vasco, congreso celebrado en París entre los días 23 de septiembre y 1 de octubre de 1956. Archivo Histórico del Gobierno Vasco. Fondo del Departamento de Presidencia, 1956–1956. Titular: Archivo del Nacionalismo Vasco. Fondo: Partido Nacionalista Vasco. Euskadiko Artxibo Historikoa, Bilbao, Basque Country, SP.

Index

Figures and tables are indicated by f or t following the page number. End note information is indicated by n and note number following the page number.

100 símbolos vascos (Rubio), 91

Abellán, José Luis, xv, 14
Aberri (Motherland), 17
Aberri Aldez (For the Motherland), 17
Aberrimin (Homesickness) (San Martin), 98–99
Acción Nacionalista (Nationalist Action), 17
Acillona, Mercedes, 103
Aesop, 62
Agirre, Domingo, 91
Agirre, José Antonio
    Basque nationalism and, 13, 14, 29, 53, 105
    cultural rebirth efforts of, 19
    as *Euzko-Gogoa* subscriber, 41
    Zaitegi and, 24, 28–29, 45
Agirre, José María ("Xabier Lizardi"), 12–13, 58, 73, 104
Agirre, Tomas ("Barrensoro"), 37
Agirre, Txomin, 38, 84, 86
Aitor, 90–91, 92
Aïtor - Légende Cantabre (Aitor, the Cantabrian Legend) (Chaho), 91
Aitorren izkuntz zarra (Andonegi), 91
Aitzol (José Ariztimuño), 12, 50–51, 58
Aizpurua, Mikel, 56
Akelarre (Coven) (Mirande), 76
Aldekoa, Iñaki, 12, 14, 37, 39, 51, 73
Alonso, Fernando, 106
Alos-Torrea (The Tower of Alos) (Etxaide), xiv, 38

Altube, Belen, 7–8
Altube, Seber, xiii
Altuna, Patxi, 22
Alvarez, Amaia, 78–79
Álvarez, Federico, 103
Álvarez, José, 13–14
Álvarez Enparantza, José Luis ("Txillardegi"), 26, 36–38, 44, 59, 96
Ama! (Mother!) (Etxaniz), 88
Amayur (Amaiur) (Etxaide), 99
"Amerika-Erdi ta Karibe'ko VI'garren Olinpiar Yolasak" (6th Caribbean Olympic Games), 85
Ametzaga, Bingen, xvi–xvii, 68t–69t, 72t
Ami Vasco (Ibero), 22
Amorrortu, Estibaliz, 9
"Anai-arteko gudatean" (The War Between Brothers) (Jauregi Jautarkol), 88
Anaitasuna (Brotherhood), xiv, 41
Anderson, Benedict, xiii, xvii–xviii, 1, 2–3, 17, 28, 50, 98–99, 109
Andonegi, Ziriako, 88, 90–91
Apalategui, Father, 22
Aralar, 35
Arana, Sabino
    on Basque language, 8–9, 11, 81
    Basque nationalism and, 10–11, 22, 28, 35, 62, 80, 81, 101–2
    Euzko-Gogoa and, 43, 50, 88
    Motherland image by, 10, 101

writings of, 35
Arangio'ko basalorea (The Wild Flower of
  Arangi) (Etxaide), 77
Arantzazu: Euskal sinesmenaren poema
  (Arantzazu: The Poem of Basque Belief)
  (Mitxelena), xiv, 37–38
Arbelbide, Xipri, 16–17
Aresti, Gabriel, xiii, 37, 59, 61, 70*t*
Aresti, Nerea, 81, 84, 87, 88
Aretxaga, Begoña, 84
Argarate, Erraimun, 30
Ariznabarreta, Larraitz, xvi
Ariztimuño, José ("Aitzol"), 12, 50–51, 58
Arozena, Andoni, 74
Arriandiaga, Imanol, 76–77
Arrieta, Leyre, 11, 44, 83, 97
Arritokieta (Julene Azpeitia), 79, 82, 83, 108
Arrue, Antonio, 59
Arruti, Domingo, 37
Arrutza, Mike, 70*t*
Artetxe, Karmele, 30
Artxanda (Unzueta), 80–81
Ascunce, José Ángel, xv–xvi, 15–16
Atxaga, Mikel, 78
Aulestia, Gorka, xiv, 14, 15, 107
Auñemendiko lorea (The Flower of the
  Pyrenees) (Agirre), 91
Aurre-Apraiz, Balendin, 89, 98, 102
Azkue, Resurrección María de, 8–10, 11, 57
Azpeitia, Julene ("Arritokieta"), 79, 82, 83, 108
Azurmendi, Joxe, 10, 41, 60, 61, 74, 97

Barandiaran, José Miguel, 63, 77
Barandiaran, Miren, 17
Baroja, Pío, 63
Barrensoro (Tomas Agirre), 37
Basque Country
  cultural rebirth of (*see* cultural rebirth)
  demographic changes in, 7–8
  Euzko-Gogoa on (*see Euzko-Gogoa*)
  geography and provinces of, vii, ix*f*
  as God's beloved country, 73–74
  historical context in (*see* historical context)
  imagined community of (*see* imagined
    community)
  language of (*see* Basque language)
  as Motherland, 10, 87–90, 101
  nationalism of (*see* Basque nationalism)
Basque language
  Basque university and, 2, 23, 25, 30, 55–56,
    61, 104–5
  education and, 2, 55–56, 62, 78, 79, 82–83,
    107 (*see also* Basque university *subentry*)
  Euskaltzaindia for (*see* Euskaltzaindia)
  Euzkaltzaleak promoting, 11–13, 78, 104
  Euzko-Gogoa and, xii–xiv, 1–3, 5–6, 10,
    18–20, 23–25, 28–30, 37, 51–73, 74–76,
    94–95, 100–109 (*see also Euzko-Gogoa*)
  generational break in, 53
  historical context for, 7–13, 8*t*, 14, 16–18,
    19–20
  imagined community and, 51–73
  intellectual level of, 58–59, 73, 104–5
  late 1950s Basque context for, 42–44
  literary publications in, xiv–xv, 4–5, 16–17,
    37–38, 42 (*see also Euzko-Gogoa*)
  nationalism and, 2–3, 5, 12, 44, 51–55, 62,
    90–97, 100–103, 106–7
  persecution of, 1, 4, 6, 14, 51, 52–54, 75–76, 94
  politics and, 23, 51–52, 95–97, 106–7
  postcolonial theory on, 4–5
  religion and, 23, 62–63, 74–76
  standardization of, 9–12, 37, 56–59, 73, 104–7
  stigmatization of, 54–55
  translations into, 23, 30, 43, 55, 59–73,
    67*t*–72*t*, 104
  women and, 78–79, 81, 82–85, 87, 88
  Zaitegi and, 22–25, 28, 37, 42, 52–53, 55–59,
    72–73, 94, 96, 100–109
Basque nationalism
  culture and, xvi, 2–3, 19
  education and, 2, 62
  Euzko-Gogoa and, 2, 5–6, 19, 28, 34–35, 44,
    51–55, 90–103, 106–7
  exiles maintaining, xvi
  historical context for, 10–12, 17, 19
  imagined community and, 2–3, 50, 51–55,
    90–103
  language and, 2–3, 5, 12, 44, 51–55, 62, 90–97,
    100–103, 106–7

late 1950s changes to, 44
literary publications supporting, 17 (*see also Euzko-Gogoa*)
national identity and, 2, 95–100
politics and, 9–11, 13–14, 28, 34–35, 44–45, 78, 95–100
religion and, 91, 102
symbols of, 28
women and, 11, 78, 79–87, 90, 109
Zaitegi and, 22
Basques (The Basques), 17
Basque university, 2, 23, 25, 30, 46n11, 55–56, 61, 104–5
Basque World Congress, 19
Basterretxea, Nestor, 107
Baudelaire, Charles, 59, 61
Begoña'ko Ama neskutz bizkaitarren zaindarijari (To the Virgin of Begoña protector of the Bizkaians) (G.E.A.), 89
Beiak (Cows) (Mirande), 77
Belaustegigoitia sisters, 85
Beltza, 8, 13, 14
Benavente, Jacinto, 63
Blot, Jacques, 35
Bonaparte, Louis-Lucien, 9
Branka (Prow), 17
Bullen, Margaret, 84

Californiako Eskual Herria (The Basque Country of California), 16–17
Calleja, Seve, 62, 63
Campión, Arturo, 8–9, 63–64
Cantemus Domino (Let Us Sing unto the Lord) (Arriandiaga), 76–77
censorship
  Euzko-Gogoa challenges due to, 25, 41, 43
  Euzko-Gogoa to combat, 1, 18, 52, 109
  literary publications and, xiv, xvii, 17, 37, 62, 107
Chaho, Agustin, 91
children's literature, 62–63
Chueca, Josu, 56
church, 74–76. *See also* religion
Collodi, Carlo, 62
Costa i Llobera, Miguel, 64

costumbrista novels, 37–38, 39, 86, 90
cultural rebirth, 21–46
  beginning of, 18
  Euzko-Gogoa role in, xi–xiii, xv, xvii, 2–6, 16, 18, 21–46, 104–7
  historical context for, 11–12, 15–20 (*see also* historical context)
  imagined community and (*see* imagined community)
  language and (*see* Basque language)
  late 1950s changes in, 42–46
  nationalism and, xvi, 2–3, 19 (*see also* Basque nationalism)
  postcolonial theory on, 4–5
  post-War of 1936, xi–xiii
  Zaitegi's personal history influencing, 21–26

Deadarra: Guda-osteko gaztediari (The Call: To the Postwar Youth) (Aurre-Apraiz), 98
decolonization, 5, 93–94
Delgado, Luisa Elena, 53
del Valle, Teresa, 84, 90, 109
Denez, Per, 64
Diaz Egurbide, Jon, xvii, 23, 40
Donostiar baten azkena (The Last of a Native from San Sebastian) (Aurre-Apraiz), 102

EAB (Emakume Abertzale Batza, Association of Nationalist Women), 11, 78, 79, 81, 82
EAJ-PNV. *See* Euzko Alderdi Jeltzalea-Partido Nacionalista Vasco
education
  Basque language and, 2, 55–56, 62, 78, 79, 82–83, 107 (*see also* Basque university subentry)
  Basque university for, 2, 23, 25, 30, 46n11, 55–56, 61, 104–5
  religion and, 76
  women and, 78, 79, 82–83
  Zaitegi's history of, 22–23
Egan (Flying), xiv–xv, 37, 39, 40, 42–43, 66, 106
Egaña, Gotzon, 86–87
Eguna (Day), 37
Ekin, xiv, 18

ELA Euzko Langille Askatasuna (Basque Workers Solidarity), 30
Eleizalde, Koldobika, 99
Emakume Abertzale Batza (EAB, Association of Nationalist Women), 11, 78, 79, 81, 82
Emakume batek (Karmele Errazti), 79, 81–82, 83, 108
"Erbestean aritza" (The Oak of Exile) (Zaitegi), 49
Eresi (Funeral March) (Mirande), 97
Eresoinka (Singing with footsteps), 19
Erkiaga, Eusebio, 72*t*
Errandonea, Father, 22
Erraondoko azken danbolinteroa (The Last Drummer of Erraondo) (Campión), 63
Errazti, Karmele ("Etxakin" or "Emakume batek"), 79, 81–82, 83, 108
Errexil, 88
Erri (Country), 17
Estefanía, Father, 22
ETA (*Euskadi ta Askatasuna*, Basque Country and Freedom), 37, 44, 60, 61, 99, 109
Etxaide, Jon, xiv, 25, 26, 38, 70*t*, 77, 99
Etxakin (Karmele Errazti), 79, 81–82, 83, 108
Etxaniz, Nemesio, 26, 62, 65, 71*t*, 88, 92
Etxaniz, Xabier, 62
Etxebarria, Igone, 79–80
Etxeberria, Frantzisko, 72*t*
Europako erri zaarrena (The Oldest Country in Europe) (Hilckman), 64
Euskadi ta Askatasuna (ETA, Basque Country and Freedom), 37, 44, 60, 61, 99, 109
Euskaldunak (The Basques) (Orixe), xiv, 12, 26, 38, 85–86
Euskal-egazti (Basque-Bird) (Etxaniz), 92
Euskal Elerti Bazkuna (Basque Literature Association), 22
Euskaltzaindia (Royal Academy of Basque Language)
  Basque language meeting by, xiv, 107
  Euzko-Gogoa criticism of, 100–103
  founding and purpose of, 9, 56, 63
  standardization stance of, 57, 59, 106
  women in, 82
  Zaitegi letters archived in, 43

Euskera maitea (Beloved Basque Language) (Andonegi), 88, 90–91
Eusko Ikaskuntza (Basque Studies Society), 56
Euzkaltzaleak, 11–13, 78, 104
Euzkeltzale batzuen azkena (The End of Some Basques) (Aurre-Apraiz), 102
"Euzkeraren alde" (In Favour of the Basque Language) (Kerexeta), 76
Euzko Alderdi Jeltzalea-Partido Nacionalista Vasco (EAJ-PNV, Basque Nationalist Party)
  Basque language and, 100–103, 106
  historical influence of, 9, 10, 11, 13, 14, 17–18
  literary publications of, 17–18
  political alliances of, 96–97, 99
  union of, 30
  women and, 84 (*see also* Emakume Abertzale Batza)
  Zaitegi and, 24, 45
Euzko-Deya (The Basque Call), 17
Euzko-Enda (Basque Race), 17
Euzko-Gogoa
  aldizkariak (magazines) referenced in, 31–34, 31*t*–33*t*
  Basque language and, xii–xiv, 1–3, 5–6, 10, 18–20, 23–25, 28–30, 37, 51–73, 74–76, 94–95, 100–109 (*see also* Basque language)
  Basque nationalism and, 2, 5–6, 19, 28, 34–35, 44, 51–55, 90–103, 106–7
  covers and design of, 34–36, 34*f*, 36*f*
  cultural rebirth with (*see* cultural rebirth)
  description of, 27–39, 103–9
  end of, 39–42, 45, 106, 109
  exiles as writers of, xii–xiii, 16, 18–19, 27, 30, 36, 49–50, 103–4, 108 (*see also specific writers*)
  financing of, 25, 30, 40–41, 44
  founding and purpose of, xii–xiv, 3, 5, 7, 16, 18–20, 24–26, 54, 104, 108 (*see also* Zaitegi, Jokin)
  generations of writers for, 36–40, 44–45, 57, 96, 108
  historical context for (*see* historical context)
  imagined community created in (*see* imagined community)

Index 129

importance of, xiii, xv
introduction section of, 27–28
*irakurlearen txokoa (*readers comments)
  section of, 31, 34, 35
late 1950s Basque context for, 42–46
politics and, 28–30, 34–35, 34f, 37, 41, 43–45,
  60–61, 64–65, 95–100
principles to examine, xvii–xviii, 1–6
publishing and distribution of, xiii, 25–26,
  27, 27t, 40–46
readers/subscribers to, 40, 73
religion and, 62–63, 65, 73–77
research on, xvi–xviii, 103
title of, xii, 43, 109
topics in, 29–31, 29t, 43, 56, 105
translations in/of, 23, 30, 43, 55, 59–73,
  67t–72t, 104
women and, 65, 77–90, 108–9
Euzko Irakastola Nagusia (Superior Basque
  School), 46n11
Evangeline (Longfellow, translated Zaitegi), 18
exiles
  Basque nationalism maintained by, xvi
  Basque World Congress for, 19
  cultural rebirth by, 18–19 (*see also* cultural
    rebirth)
  diasporic communities of, 14–16, 17
  Euzko-Gogoa writers as, xii–xiii, 16, 18–19,
    27, 30, 36, 49–50, 103–4, 108 (*see also*
    Zaitegi, Jokin)
  imagined community of, 49–50, 103–4 (*see
    also* imagined community)
  literature influenced by, xv–xvi, 1, 15–19, 49
  suffering and struggles of, 15–16, 18–19,
    103–4
  War of 1936 creating, 14
  women as, 79–80, 81, 82, 83
  Zaitegi as, xiii, 18–19, 40–46, 60, 103
Ezcurra, Andrés Townsend, 94
Ez Dok Amairu (The Curse of Number 13 is
  Broken), 107

Fanon, Frantz, xviii, 4–5, 28, 51, 52, 80
forced migrants. *See* exiles
Franco, Francisco and regime

Basque cultural rebirth despite (*see* cultural
  rebirth)
Basque language persecution under, 1, 4, 6,
  14, 51, 52–54, 75–76, 94
censorship under (*see* censorship)
Euzko-Gogoa publishing and, 40–41, 43
exiles under (*see* exiles)
political coup d'état by, 13–14
religion and, 23–24, 74–76, 77, 102
removal of, hope for, xiv, 97
Fraterrigo, Elizabeth, xviii, 4, 36
Frente Popular (Popular Front), 13
fueros (Basque laws), 10, 22, 28, 52, 104

Garate, Gotzon, 22, 23, 64, 72t
Garibay, Esteban de, 74
Garoa (Fern) (Agirre), 86
Gartzia, Pruden, 104
Gau donea (Holy Night) (Lagerlöf), 65
Gaurik gogorrena (The Hardest Night) (Aurre-
  Apraiz), 89
G.E.A., 89
Gellner, Ernest, xvii, 1–2, 55
Gerediaga, 107
Gernika (Gernika), 17
"Gernikako Arbola" (The Tree of Gernika)
  (Iparragirre), 92
Gifford, Justin, xviii, 4, 36
gipuzkera osatua (enhanced Gipuzcoan), 12,
  57, 73
Goethe, Johann Wolfgang von, 60
Goikoetxea, Jon, 22
Goikoetxea, Juan Iñazio, 26
Goiri, Sabino Arana, xii
"Goizeko izarra" (The Morning Star)
  (Azpeitia), 82
Goytino, Jean Pierre, 16–17
Guatemala
  Basque women in, 85
  Euzko-Gogoa in, xiii, xv, 25, 27, 30–31, 34–35,
    34f, 40–42 (*see also Euzko-Gogoa*)
  politics and government in, 24
  Zaitegi and exiles in, xi, xif, 18, 24–25, 41, 45
Gudari (Basque Soldier), 17
Gurpide, Pablo, 43

Gurruchaga, Ander, xvi, 76
Guruz bidea euskal-samiñaren (The Way of the Cross: the Cry of Basque Sorrow) (Mitxelena), 89
Gutun agiria (Letter Document) (Aurre-Apraiz), 102

Hacia el futuro agrario (Toward the Agrarian Future), 30–31
Haritschelhar, Jean, 9
Heine, Christian Johann Heinrich, 60
Hilckman, Anton, 64
historical context, 7–20
    Arana's influence in, 8–9, 10–11, 22
    Basque language in, 7–13, 8t, 14, 16–18, 19–20
    Basque nationalism in, 10–12, 17, 19
    Basque World Congress in, 19
    coup d'état in, 13–14
    cultural initiatives in, 11–12, 15–20 (*see also* Basque language *subentry*)
    demographic changes in, 7–8
    exiles in, 14–19
    literary publications in, 15–20 (*see also specific publications*)
    overview of, xviii
    politics in, 9–14, 17–18, 19
    Second Carlist War in, 8
    Spanish Second Republic in, 13
    War of 1936 in, 14
    women's influence in, 11
historical memory, 102

Ianko ereslari (Janko the Musician) (Sienkiewicz), 64
Ibáñez Martín, José, 43
Ibargutxi, Miren Arrate ("Miren-A"), 79, 82, 108
Ibarluzea, Miren, 66
Ibero, Evangelista de, 22
Ibiñagabeitia, Andima
    on Basque language, 28, 37, 55, 57, 73, 94, 96, 100–102
    Euzko-Gogoa translations by, 65, 68t, 69t–70t, 72t
    as *Euzko-Gogoa* writer/director, xiii, 22, 28, 36, 51, 56
    on exile, 18
    on Israel, 92
    photograph of, xif
    religion and, 73
    on women writers, 83, 84
    Zaitegi and, xi, xif, 22, 26, 44, 45–46
ikurriña (Basque flag), 28
imagined community, 49–109
    Arana's contributions to, 10, 50, 62, 80, 81, 88, 101–2
    Basque language and, 51–73
    Basque nationalism and, 2–3, 50–55, 90–103
    Euzko-Gogoa creation of, xiii, 1–4, 19, 28, 41–42, 45, 49–109
    Motherland for, 10, 87–90, 101
    overview of, xviii, 49–51, 103–9
    real community vs., 41–42, 95–109
    religion and, 73–77
    research on, xvii–xviii, 103
    women and, 77–90, 108–9
immigration, 7–8, 84
El INFOP: esperanza de Guatemala (INFOP: the Hope of Guatemala), 30
Insausti, Josu, 62, 65, 69t, 94
Intxausti, Joseba, xv, 24, 34, 38, 107
Iñurrieta, Engratzi ("Sagar-Erreka"), 79, 82, 108
Iparragirre, Jose Maria, 90, 91–92
Ipui Onac (Good Stories) (Mogel), 62
Irazusta, Joseba Andoni, 18, 96
Irigoien, Alfonso, 11, 70t
Irrintzi (Basque Scream "Neigh"), 17
Irujo, Xabier, xvi–xvii, 6
Israel, 92–93
Iturrioz, Antonio, 70t
Itxarkundia (Hope) (Arana), 35
Itxaropena, xiv
Itxartu, euzko-alabea (Wake up Basque Daughter) (Unzueta), 80
Itzaltzu'ko koblaria (The Bard of Itzaltzu) (Campión), 63
Itzulpengintzaren erreprestazioa euskal literatura garaikidean (Representation of Translation in the Contemporary Basque Literature) (Ibarluzea), 66
Izkillu deya (Weapon Call) (Eleizalde), 99

Izkuntza eta abenda (Language and Race) (Campión), 63–64
Iztueta, Paulo
  on 1950s significance, 107
  on Arana and nationalism, 10
  on *Euzko-Gogoa*, xvi, 25–26, 40, 42, 52, 59, 61
  on exile, xvi
  on translations, 59, 61
  on Zaitegi, xvii, 10, 22–23, 42

Jacobson, Matthew, 17
Jakin (Knowledge), xiv, 37, 40, 41, 106
Jauregi, A., 71t
Jauregi Jautarkol, Koldo, 88
Jesusen Biotzaren Deya (The Call of Jesus's Heart), 22
Jiménez, Juan Ramón, 63
Joanixio (Johnny) (Irazusta), 18
Juaristi, Jon, 64
Juaristi, Migel, 72t

Kafka, Franz, 60–61
Karmel (Carmelite), 41
Kartak nola idatzi euskaraz? (How to write letters in Basque?) (Etxaniz), 62
Kerexeta, Jaime, 76, 84–85
Kintana, Jurgi, 9
Kortazar, Jon, 16
Kristau-ikasbidea bertsotan (Christian Doctrine in Verse), 62
Krutwig, Federico, xiii, 26, 36–37, 54, 57, 104, 106

Labaien, Antonio Maria, xiv, 68t, 84, 93, 97, 103
Lagerlöf, Selma, 65, 108
Larrakoetxea, Bedita, 39, 61, 72t, 94
Larrañaga, Eladio, 61, 68t
Larrañaga, Guillermo, 22, 36, 62, 71t
Larrañaga, Policarpo de, 11
Lauaxeta (Esteban Urkiaga), 22, 73, 104
Lekuona, Manuel, 12
Lete, Xabier, 12
Leturiaren egunkari ezkutua (Leturia's Secret Diary) (Txillardegi), 38
El libro negro del euskera (The Black Book of the Basque Language) (Torrealdai), 54

Lizardi (José María Agirre), 12–13, 58, 73, 104
Llona, Miren, 11, 89
Lopez-Mendizabal, Ixaka, 62
Loretxo (Flower) (Arruti), 37

Maitasun eta erio kantua (An Indian Study of Love and Death) (Nivedita), 65, 77
Maitaxun ixilla (Silent Love) (Mistral), 65
Mañari, Errose, 83
Manciet, Bernart, 64
Markuleta, Gerardo, 104
memory, historical, 102
Mess, Ludger, 29
Mintegi, Laura, 82
Mirande, Jon
  Euzko-Gogoa translations by, 60–61, 67t–68t, 70t
  as *Euzko-Gogoa* writer, xiii, 26, 36, 38, 45–46, 56, 76–77
  politics and, 60, 97–98
Miren-A (Miren Arrate Ibargutxi), 79, 82, 108
Mistral, Gabriela, 65, 108
Mitxelena, Koldo, xiv, 38, 39, 59, 66, 105–6
Mitxelena, Salbatore, 26, 36, 37–38, 89
Mix Garai, Jon, 101
Mogel, Bixenta, 62
Mokoroa, Justo M., 69t
Mola, Emilio, 13
Monzón, Telésforo de, xiii, 18, 55
Mother, Holy, 88–89, 108
motherhood, 79, 80–81, 82–85, 87–90, 108–9
Motherland, image of, 10, 87–90, 101
Mujika, Luis Mari, 62, 72t
Mujika, Plácido, 22
mythology, 76–77

Nación Vasca (Basque Nation), 17
nationalism. *See* Basque nationalism
Ninyoles, Rafael, 1
Nivedita, Sister, 65, 77, 108
Noni eta Mani (Noni and Mani), 63
Nuñez-Betelu, Maite, 11, 80, 81, 82

Oficina de Prensa de Euskadi (OPE, press office of the Basque Country), 26

Oiartzabal, Martin, 57–58, 64, 71*t*–72*t*
Olabide, Father, 22
Olaziregi, Mari Jose, 10, 29, 37, 41, 52, 77, 91
Onaindia, Santi, xiv, 71*t*
"Opariz" (Gift) (Zaitegi), 87–88
Ormaetxea, Nikolas ("Orixe")
    on Basque language, 57–58
    as *Euzko-Gogoa* writer, xiii, 26, 36, 37, 51, 56, 57–58
    on ideal Basque woman, 85–86
    photograph of, xi*f*
    poetry and writings of, xiv, 12, 26, 38, 39, 75
    on politics, 98
    religion and, 73, 75
    replacement of, as writer, 44, 105
    Zaitegi and, xi, xi*f*, 26
Ortiz-Osés, Andrés, 91
Ortzi'ren ttunttuna (Ortzi's Drum) (Mirande), 76
Otaegi, Lourdes, 12, 13, 61, 77
Oteiza, Jorge, 94, 107

paganism, 76–77
passports, Basque, 24
Peillen, Txomin, 26, 36
Poe, Edgar Allan, 60–61
politics
    Basque language and, 23, 51–52, 95–97, 106–7
    Basque nationalism and, 9–11, 13–14, 28, 34–35, 44–45, 78, 95–100 (*see also* Basque nationalism)
    Euzko-Gogoa and, 28–30, 34–35, 34*f*, 37, 41, 43–45, 60–61, 64–65, 95–100
    historical context of, 9–14, 17–18, 19
    literary publications addressing, 17–18, 78 (*see also Euzko-Gogoa*)
    neutrality toward, 12, 28, 95
    women and, 11, 78, 79–87, 90, 109
    Zaitegi and, 24, 28–29, 34, 41, 43, 45, 64, 95, 97, 99–103
postcolonial theory, 4–5
Preston, Paul, 51

Quiton arrebarekin (In Quito with My Sister) (Orixe), 26, 75

religion
    Basque Country as God's beloved country, 73–74
    Basque language and, 23, 62–63, 74–76
    Basque nationalism and, 91, 102
    the church and, 74–76
    historical context for, 8, 10, 11, 13, 22
    imagined community and, 73–77
    mythology, paganism, and, 76–77
    translations on, 62–63, 65
    women and, 81, 82, 86–87, 88–90, 108
    Zaitegi and, 22–24, 43, 73
Romanticism, 60
Rubio, Coro, 91

Sagar-Erreka (Engratzi Iñurrieta), 79, 82, 108
Said, Edward W., 16, 18
Sánchez Albornoz, Claudio, 74
San Martin, Juan, 37, 58, 72*t*, 98–99
San Miguel, María Luisa, xvi
Santa Maria Goretti (Saint Mary Goretti) (Sorrain), 62
Sarobe, Francisco, 22
Saroyan, William, 62
Sarrionandia, Joseba, 15
Second Carlist War, 8
Shakespeare, William, 55, 61
Sienkiewicz, Henryk, 64
Sinisten dut askatasunean (I Believed in Freedom) (Zaitegi), 64
Smith, Adam D., xvii, 1–2, 28
Sophocles, 2, 55
Sorrain, Antonio, 62, 69*t*
Sortzez garbiari (To the Pure from Birth) (Aurre-Apraiz), 89
Spanish Civil War. *See* War of 1936
Spanish Second Republic, 13, 53
"Staël anderea (1766–1817)" (Madame de Staël, 1766-1817) (Zaitegi), 86
Sudupe, Pako, xvii, 42
symbols, nationalist, 28

Tabori, Paul, xiii
Taur, Norbert, 55–56
Thiong'o, Ngũgĩ wa, xviii, 5, 51, 52, 79, 94

Index

Toledo, Ana, 38, 86
Torrealdai, Joan Mari, xv, 1, 18, 25, 37, 42, 54, 107
Tovar, Antonio, 43
Trabudua, Polixene, 81, 89
translations, 23, 30, 43, 55, 59–73, 67*t*–72*t*, 104
Txillardegi (José Luis Álvarez Enparantza), 26, 36–38, 44, 59, 96

Ubico, Jorge, 24
Ugalde, Martin, xv, xvi, 8, 18
Ugalde, Mercedes, 11, 34, 78, 83, 84, 90
Uhland, Ludwig, 60
Unamuno, Miguel de, 8
unions, 30
university, Basque, 2, 23, 25, 30, 46n11, 55–56, 61, 104–5
University of Nevada, Center for Basque Studies, 56, 105
Unzueta, Sorne ("Utarsus"), 79–81, 108
Uranzadi Digital, 16
Urkiaga, Esteban ("Lauaxeta"), 22, 73, 104
Urrundik (From Afar) (Monzón), 18
Urrutia, Gotzon, 54, 55, 74
Urrutia, Iñigo, 6
Urtzi, 76–77
Utarsus (Sorne Unzueta), 79–81, 108
Uztaro (Harvest Time) (Agirre), 37

Vasconia (Krutwig), 106
Velez de Mendizabal, Josemari, xvi, 24, 25, 40, 43, 44
Verlaine, Paul, 59, 61
Villasante, Luis, 13
Virgin Mary, 88–90, 108
Virgin of Begoña, 89

War of 1936
  Basque university closure due to, 46n11, 56
  censorship after (*see* censorship)
  cultural rebirth following, xi–xii (*see also* cultural rebirth)
  exile following (*see* exiles)
  historical context of, 14
  nationalism and writings on, 102
  religion and writings on, 75

terminology for, vii
women's losses in, 80–81, 83, 88
women
  archetypal nationalist, 79–87, 90, 109
  Basque language and, 78–79, 81, 82–85, 87, 88
  education and, 78, 79, 82–83
  historical influence of, 11
  imagined community and, 77–90, 108–9
  motherhood of, 79, 80–81, 82–85, 87–90, 108–9
  politics and, 11, 78, 79–87, 90, 109
  prejudice toward, 84–85, 87
  religion and, 81, 82, 86–87, 88–90, 108
  translations of writings of, 65
  as writers, 65, 77–85, 90, 108–9
Woolf, Virginia, 79

Xabiertxo (Little Xavier) (Ugalde), 18
Xabiertxo (Lopez-Mendizabal), 62
Xemein, Keperin, 36, 58, 81–82

Yeiki Yeiki (Wake Up Wake Up) (Mirande), 97–98
young adult literature, 62

Zabal (Wide), xvi
Zaitegi, Jokin
  Basque language and, 22–25, 28, 37, 42, 52–53, 55–59, 72–73, 94, 96, 100–109 (*see also under Euzko-Gogoa*)
  Basque university support by, 23, 25, 30, 56
  biography of, xvi
  critiques of, 39, 40, 105–6
  cultural rebirth influence of, 19, 21–46 (*see also* cultural rebirth)
  description and personal history of, 21–26, 45
  Euzko-Gogoa finances and, 25, 30, 40–41, 44
  Euzko-Gogoa founding by, xii–xiii, 3, 5, 18–20, 24–26, 51, 104, 108
  Euzko-Gogoa translations by, 60, 67*t*, 68*t*, 71*t*
  as *Euzko-Gogoa* writer, 26, 36
  historical context and, 7, 10, 18–20
  late 1950s Basque changes affecting, 42–46, 106
  pen names of, 26
  photograph of, xi*f*

politics and, 24, 28–29, 34, 41, 43, 45, 64, 95, 97, 99–103
religion and, 22–24, 43, 73
relocation and forced migration of, xiii, 18–19, 40–46, 60, 103
research on contributions of, xvii, xviii
on women images, 85–86, 87–88

writings of, 18, 49 (*see also Euzko-Gogoa*)
Zatarain, Anbrozio, 60, 68*t*
Zinkunegi, Joseba, 71*t*
Zuazo, Koldo, 9, 59
Zulaika, Joseba, 54, 84, 89, 99
Zumeta, Jose Luis, 107
Zurdo, David Mota, 19

www.ingramcontent.com/pod-product-compliance
Lightning Source LLC
Chambersburg PA
CBHW071849230426
43671CB00012B/2124